Financing Higher Education in Africa

Financing Higher Education in Africa

THE WORLD BANK
Washington, D.C.

© 2010 The International Bank for Reconstruction and Development / The World Bank

1818 H Street NW
Washington DC 20433
Telephone: 202-473-1000
Internet: www.worldbank.org
E-mail: feedback@worldbank.org

All rights reserved

1 2 3 4 13 12 11 10

This volume is a product of the staff of the International Bank for Reconstruction and Development / The World Bank. The findings, interpretations, and conclusions expressed in this volume do not necessarily reflect the views of the Executive Directors of The World Bank or the governments they represent.

The World Bank does not guarantee the accuracy of the data included in this work. The boundaries, colors, denominations, and other information shown on any map in this work do not imply any judgement on the part of The World Bank concerning the legal status of any territory or the endorsement or acceptance of such boundaries.

Rights and Permissions

The material in this publication is copyrighted. Copying and/or transmitting portions or all of this work without permission may be a violation of applicable law. The International Bank for Reconstruction and Development / The World Bank encourages dissemination of its work and will normally grant permission to reproduce portions of the work promptly.

For permission to photocopy or reprint any part of this work, please send a request with complete information to the Copyright Clearance Center Inc., 222 Rosewood Drive, Danvers, MA 01923, USA; telephone: 978-750-8400; fax: 978-750-4470; Internet: www.copyright.com.

All other queries on rights and licenses, including subsidiary rights, should be addressed to the Office of the Publisher, The World Bank, 1818 H Street NW, Washington, DC 20433, USA; fax: 202-522-2422; e-mail: pubrights@worldbank.org.

ISBN-13: 978-0-8213-8334-6
eISBN: 978-0-8213-8337-7
DOI: 10.1596/978-0-8213-8334-6

Cataloging-in-publication data has been requested
Library of Congress Control Number: 2010926044

Cover design by Quantum Think

Contents

Foreword		*xiii*
Acknowledgments		*xvii*
Abbreviations		*xix*
Chapter 1	**Introduction**	1
	Rising Social Demand and Sustainable Financing	1
	Main Features of Current Funding Policies and Practices	3
	Tools for Financially Sustainable Policies	6
	The Implementation of Financing Reforms	9
	Purpose and Organization of the Study	10
Chapter 2	**Rising Social Demand and the Challenge of Sustainable Financing**	13
	Current Demand for Higher Education and Government Funding Capacity	16
	Public Resources per Student and Efforts to Raise Quality	20

v

	Projected Demand for Higher Education and Public Financing	27
	Notes	35
	References	37
Chapter 3	**Main Features of Current Funding Policies and Practices**	**39**
	Operating Budget Allocation Practices	39
	Investment Budget Allocation Practices	47
	Budget Management Practices and the Optimal Use of Available Resources	49
	Private Funding for Tertiary Education	55
	Student Financial Assistance	74
	Loan Programs	77
	External Assistance to Higher Education	94
	Foundation Support	105
	External Aid for Research and Development	106
	Notes	110
	References	112
Chapter 4	**Tools for Financially Sustainable Tertiary Education Policies**	**119**
	Improving the Management of Public Financing	120
	Managing the Trends in Student Flows	131
	Developing Distance Education	136
	Mobilizing Private Resources	136
	Streamlining Student Support Services	144
	Promoting the Private Sector	147
	Rethinking Research Funding	150
	Combining Tools for Financially Sustainable Tertiary Education Policies	151
	Notes	153
	References	153
Chapter 5	**Ensuring the Successful Implementation of Financing Reforms**	**157**
	Addressing the Political Feasibility of Reforms	158
	Putting in Place Favorable Governance Arrangements	163

	Strengthening Planning and Management Capacity	166
	Assessing Policy Options to Anticipate Possible Consequences	168
	References	170

Boxes

3.1	Budget Allocation Practices in Mali	40
3.2	Line Item Budgeting in Uganda	43
3.3	Normative Input-based Budgeting in Nigeria	44
3.4	Formula Funding in South Africa	46
3.5	Research Funding in Nigeria	55
3.6	Research Funding for Agriculture	56
3.7	A Financial Revolution: Makerere University in Uganda	64
3.8	Tuition Fees in Public Higher Education Institutions in Benin	66
3.9	The Cost of Studies Abroad: The Case of Mauritius	73
3.10	The Nature of Direct and Indirect Aid to Higher Education	97
3.11	Building ICT Capacities in Africa	100
3.12	Support for Higher Education	101
3.13	How Many African Students Return to Their Country of Origin after Completing Their Studies?	105
3.14	The National Research Fund and Modalities of Funding in Mozambique	108
3.15	Methodological Note	109
4.1	Ghana Education Trust Fund	123
4.2	Emergency Universities Program in Côte d'Ivoire	124
4.3	Mozambique's Competitive Fund for Tertiary Education	128
4.4	International Experience with Competitive Funds	129
4.5	A Plan for Streamlining Higher Education in Côte d'Ivoire	130
4.6	Selective Admission into Higher Education	134
4.7	A Distance Education Experiment	138
4.8	Phasing the Introduction of Cost Sharing: The Case of Tanzania	140
4.9	Some Rules for Avoiding Budget Overruns Resulting from Grants or Scholarships	145

4.10	An Alternative to Scholarships Abroad: Building and Offering Quality Local Education	146
4.11	Examples of the State's Disengagement from Housing, Catering, and Other Nonacademic Services Provided to Students	148
4.12	Development of Private Higher Education in Some African Countries	149
5.1	Consensus Building and Cost Sharing in Northern Mexico	160
5.2	Autonomy and Excellence at Work: The National School of Business Administration	165

Figures

2.1	Share of Higher Education in Current Public Expenditure on Education in African Countries, 2006 (or Closest Year)	15
2.2	Public Expenditure on Higher Education and the Form of the Education Pyramid in African Countries, 2006 (or Closest Year)	16
2.3	Change in the Number of Higher Education Students and Expenditure on Higher Education in Two Groups of African Countries, 1991–2006	18
2.4	Ratio between the Change in the Number of Higher Education Students and the Amount of Public Resources Allocated to Current Expenditure on Higher Education in African Countries, 1991–2006	19
2.5	Annual Current Public Expenditure per Student in African Countries, 2006 (or Closest Year)	23
2.6	Public Expenditure per Student and Ratio of the Number of Students to the Current Level of Public Expenditure on Higher Education in Select African Countries, 2006	24
2.7	Student-Teacher Ratio in Higher Education in Select African Countries, Public and Private Sectors Combined, 2006 (or Closest Year)	25
2.8	Change in the Number of Higher Education Students in Africa, 1982–2006 and Projected through 2015	28
2.9	Number of Students Expected in 2015 in African Countries on the Basis of Current Trends in Higher Education Growth	29

2.10	Current Expenditure on Higher Education and Public Expenditure Required to Expand Higher Education in Africa at Current Rates and Unit Costs, 2004–15	31
3.1	Share of Households in National Expenditure on Higher Education in Select African Countries, 2004 (or Closest Year)	57
3.2	Average Share of Households in National Expenditure on Education in 18 African Countries, by Level of Instruction, 2004 (or Closest Year)	58
3.3	Breakdown of Current Public Expenditure on Higher Education in Select African Countries	70
3.4	Trade-off between Social and Wage Expenditure within the Public Higher Education Budget in Select African Countries	71
3.5	Proportion of African Students Enrolled in Private Institutions, 35 Countries, 2006 (or Closest Year)	75
3.6	Distribution of Aid to Higher Education, by Region, 2002–06 Average (Commitments)	95
3.7	Aid to Education in Sub-Saharan Africa, by Level of Education, 2002–06 Average	96
3.8	Total Aid to Africa for Higher Education, Commitments, 2002–06	97
3.9	Direct Aid to Higher Education in Select African Countries, Annual Average Commitments, 2001–06	98
3.10	Direct Aid to Higher Education per Student in Select African Countries, Annual Average Commitments, 2001–06	99
3.11	Assistance from the Partnership for Higher Education in Africa, 2000–08	106
4.1	Estimated Number of Higher Education Students in Mali, Assuming Current Trends and Regulations in Secondary Education, 2005–16	133
4.2	Number of Students as a Function of Length of Studies	135
4.3	Estimated Number of Higher Education Students in Mali, Assuming Current Trends and Various Flow Management Measures, 2005–16	137
4.4	Number of Foreign Students Studying in Morocco and Number of Moroccan Students Studying Abroad, 2003–06	146

Tables

2.1	Public Expenditure on Higher Education as a Percentage of GDP, by Country Group, 1990 and 2006	14
2.2	Share of Higher Education in Current Public Expenditure on Education, by Country Group, 1990 and 2006	14
2.3	Ratio between the Increase in the Number of Higher Education Students and the Increase in Public Resources Allocated to Current Expenditure on Higher Education, by Country Group, 1991 and 2006	17
2.4	Average Gross Enrollment Ratio in 31 Sub-Saharan African Countries, by Level of Education, 1990–2005	20
2.5	Average Public Expenditure per Student in 18 Sub-Saharan African Countries, by Level of Education, 1975, 1990, and 2003	21
2.6	Annual Public Expenditure per Student, by Country Group, 1990 and 2006	21
2.7	Number of Scientific Publications and Patent Applications, by Region, 2002	26
2.8	Number of Students and Average Annual Expenditure Required to Support the Expansion of Higher Education in African Countries at Current Enrollment Rates and Unit Costs, 2004–15	32
2.9	Proportion of Senior Faculty Members in Public Higher Education Institutions in Select African Countries	34
3.1	Methods of Allocating the Higher Education Budget in Select African Countries	42
3.2	Budgeting Modalities	47
3.3	Entity in Charge of Higher Education Oversight, by Language Area	52
3.4	Types and Amounts of Tuition Fees in Public Higher Education Institutions	60
3.5	Financial Significance of Tuition Fees in Select Countries	67
3.6	Composition of Higher Education Budget, by Country Group, 2006 or Closest Year	69
3.7	Share of Scholarships Abroad in Current Higher Education Expenditures in 19 African Countries, Most Recent Year Available	72
3.8	Share of Own Resources in the Total Revenue of Public Higher Education Institutions in Select African Countries	76

3.9	Student Financial Assistance Programs in African Countries	78
3.10	Student Loan Schemes in Africa	83
3.11	Loan Recovery in Select African Countries	90
3.12	Indirect Aid to Higher Education in Select African Countries, Annual Average Commitments, 2001–06	102
3.13	Direct and Indirect Aid to Higher Education in Select African Countries, Annual Average Commitments, 2001–06	104
3.14	Targets for Expenditure on Select Sectoral Priorities	107
4.1	Advantages and Disadvantages of Various Funding Mechanisms	122
4.2	Measures for the Sustainable Financing of Higher Education	152
5.1	Changing Approaches to Financial Control in Madagascar	164

Foreword

In 2008, the World Bank published *Accelerating Catch Up—Tertiary Education for Growth in Sub-Saharan Africa,* which spelled out the case for more knowledge-intensive growth in Africa and described the critical role of higher education in this endeavor. This report demonstrated that the key for success in a globalized world lies increasingly in how effectively a country can assimilate the available knowledge and build comparative advantages in areas with good growth prospects and how it can use technology to address the most pressing environmental challenges. Higher-level institutions in Sub-Saharan Africa that are equipped to impart quality education and conduct relevant applied research can play a critical role in producing workers with the skills to assimilate technology and make effective decisions that help industry to diversify into a broader range of products. Good-quality and relevant higher education is also a key to stimulating innovations in new varieties of crops, new materials, or sources of energy that would facilitate progress toward reducing poverty, achieving food security, and improving health. However, higher-level institutions in Sub-Saharan Africa face the formidable policy challenge of balancing the need to raise educational quality with increasing social demand for access. And since the task of funding these institutions will become increasingly difficult in the years ahead, as the youth population continues to grow, each country will have to devise a financing approach to higher education development that enables it to meet the challenges.

This report is a follow-up to the 2008 study. It examines current practices in financing higher education in Sub-Saharan Africa, taking into account the significant differences that exist among countries. Drawing on experience from around the world, the report also examines the range of policy options that could be considered in tackling the financing issue.

Backed by a significant amount of new and updated data, the report concludes that in most Sub-Saharan African countries, enrollment in higher education has grown faster than financing capabilities, reaching a critical stage where the lack of resources has led to a severe decline in the quality of instruction and in the capacity to reorient focus and to innovate. Public funding in most countries is already overstretched, and alone it will not be sufficient to respond to the growing demand for access to higher education while delivering a level of quality that provides students with the skills necessary to succeed in current and future labor markets. The easy path of laissez-faire expansionism driven by supply-side pressures, which is evident in some countries, will only lead to even further deterioration.

The report also carries an encouraging message. It shows that a full range of options do exist and that some African countries and institutions have started implementing them. Private higher education is experiencing spectacular growth in Africa. Cost-sharing programs are being implemented in many universities, accompanied by student loans and financial aid for low-income students. Higher education is being diversified to offer lower cost and more effective delivery alternatives. In a few cases, impressive reforms to improve internal efficiency have been implemented, and governments are increasingly adopting more effective budget management practices.

This report makes the case for a comprehensive approach that would combine all the tools that can ensure more financially sustainable higher education systems. How the measures should be combined and the pace at which the reforms should be implemented depend on the situation and constraints specific to each country. The report also admits that reforming the financing of higher education is difficult and can generate controversies and tensions. This is why policy makers should carefully present the arguments, assess the impacts of proposed solutions, and engage in a wide consultation so that stakeholders are better informed of the link between proposed reforms and the likely improvement in teaching and learning conditions.

It is my hope that the publication of this report will enrich the ongoing debate within countries, among stakeholders, and between African countries and their development partners. Informed by global good practices, our common goal is to make higher education contribute to finding solutions to the developmental challenges facing Africa.

Yaw Ansu
Sector Director, Human Development
Africa Region

Acknowledgments

This study is the result of a collective effort. It combines several contributions from partner institutions and experts in the financing of tertiary education. The concept and outline were discussed in a meeting held in Dakar on November 2008 that gathered representatives of the United Nations Educational, Scientific, and Cultural Organization (UNESCO), Pôle de Dakar, the Association of African Universities, French Cooperation, and the World Bank. This effort was led by William Experton (World Bank) and Chloe Fevre (World Bank) and included the following contributors (in alphabetical order): Fadila Caillaud (World Bank), Borel Foko (Pôle de Dakar), Pierre Antoine Gioan (CampusFrance), Bruce Johnstone (State University of New York, or SUNY), Pamela Marcucci (SUNY), Petra Righetti (World Bank), William Saint (World Bank), and Jamil Salmi (World Bank). This study was reviewed by Peter Darvas (World Bank), Peter Materu (World Bank), Benoit Millot (World Bank), and Jee-Peng Tan (World Bank).

Abbreviations

DSPW	Department of Student Placement and Welfare
FONER	Fond National pour l'Education et la Recherche (Burkina Faso)
GDP	gross domestic product
GET	Ghana Education Trust
GNI	gross national income
HELB	Higher Education Loans Board, Kenya
HESLB	Higher Education Students Loans Board, Tanzania
ICT	information and communication technology
ICT4D	ICT for Development Project
INSCAE	School of Business Administration, Madagascar
IT	information technology
KCSE	Kenya Certificate of Secondary Education
LMD	*licence-master-doctorat*
MHEST	Ministry of Higher Education, Science, and Technology, Tanzania
MOE	Ministry of Education
MoEVT	Ministry of Education and Vocational Training, Tanzania
OECD	Organisation for Economic Co-operation and Development

QIF	Quality Enhancement and Innovation Fund, Mozambique
R&D	research and development
SFAR	Student Financing Agency for Rwanda
SLTF	Student Loan Trust Fund, Ghana
S&T	science and technology
UIS	UNESCO Institute for Statistics
UNAM	National Autonomous University of Mexico
UNESCO	United Nations Educational, Scientific, and Cultural Organization

CHAPTER 1

Introduction

Sustainable growth in Africa is contingent on the capacity of states to diversify their economies and thus train human capital that will help to carry out and support this transformation. In this process and when investment capacity is limited, higher education plays a key role in training qualified individuals who will be capable of implementing new technologies and using innovative methods to establish more efficient enterprises and institutions and thus allocate resources more effectively. Through research and increased knowledge, higher education can also help to address the challenges arising from population growth, limited arable land, endemic diseases, urbanization, energy costs, and climate change. However, in order for Sub-Saharan Africa to reap the benefits of this investment in human capital, higher education institutions must have financing to provide quality training and sound professional prospects to their students.

Rising Social Demand and Sustainable Financing

The rapid growth in the number of students is a challenge to the sustainable financing of higher education. Africa has maintained its public investment in higher education over the last 15 years, allocating approximately 0.78 percent of its gross domestic product (GDP) and around 20 percent of its current public expenditure on education to this sector. However, during this period, the total number of students pursuing higher education tripled, climbing from 2.7 million in 1991 to 9.3 million in 2006 (an annual average rate of 16 percent), while public resources allocated to current expenditure in that sector only doubled (an annual average rate of 6 percent). The situation is even more dire in the poorest countries in Africa, which allocate approximately 0.63 percent of their GDP to higher education and where during the 1991–2006 period the number of students quadrupled, while available public resources in general only increased by at most 75 percent.

The decline in public expenditure per student is having an adverse impact on the quality and relevance of education programs. Africa is the only region in the world that has experienced a decrease in the volume of current public expenditure per student (30 percent over the last 15 years). Yet average annual current public expenditure per student remains relatively high (approximately US$2,000 in 2006), which is more than twice the amount allocated in non-African developing countries. Annual public expenditure per student in Africa therefore represents nearly three times GDP per capita, compared to only one-third in Organisation for Economic Co-operation and Development (OECD) countries and 1.2 times GDP per capita at the global level. The impact of the decline in public resources on the functioning of higher education varies from country to country. It is however stronger in countries that have a low rate of public expenditure per student (some 15 countries spend less than US$1,000 per student) and that must cope with a sharp increase in the number of students. Admitting an ever-increasing number of students results in a trade-off that often occurs at the expense of quality and particularly at the expense of expenditure on wages. Universities are finding it increasingly difficult to maintain a teaching staff, lecture halls are overcrowded, and buildings are falling into disrepair, teaching equipment is not replenished, investment in research and in training for new teachers is insufficient, and many teachers must supplement their incomes by providing services to the private sector. At worst, the lack of resources may lead to student protests and strikes that jeopardize the completion of the academic year.

If current trends continue apace, the total number of students for the entire African continent could reach between 18 million and 20 million by 2015. The level of expenditure could be 75 percent higher than the volume of public resources that may be mobilized. The number of teachers required would need to double, from a total of approximately 456,000 in 2006 to 908,000 by 2015. It will be even more difficult for these countries to retain a sufficient number of senior faculty members, who are necessary for the conduct of research, the improvement in the scientific and pedagogical quality of instruction, and the preparation of future generations of teachers and researchers. Indeed, the level of effort devoted to research has been inadequate to train a sufficient number of doctoral students. The investment required over the 2006–2015 period to increase the capacity of current institutions (classrooms, libraries, laboratories, workshops, and lecture halls), establishing new institutions that are better distributed across the territory, and improving administrative and teaching materials is estimated at approximately US$45 billion (in 2006 dollars) for public higher education as a whole, of which US$20 billion is for low-income countries. However, very few countries in Africa have the leeway to increase the public financing of higher education. Their tax base is generally low and the share of the budget that could be earmarked for higher education is hard to increase when most of these countries must also meet a high demand for access to secondary education and several of them are far from achieving universal primary education.

International aid in support of higher education is on average US$600 million annually, or one-quarter of all international aid to the education sector in Sub-Saharan Africa. This relatively low share reflects the current emphasis given by most donors on the development of basic education and the achievement of Education for All. In addition to the small amounts of aid, two main factors limit the impact of aid. First, only 26 percent of aid to higher education goes directly to African universities and research centers. The remainder is provided through scholarships abroad or is accounted for by directly imputing student costs in the donors' universities. Second, aid is highly fragmented, owing partly to the lack of donor coordination. On the other hand, aid is increasingly supporting the education sector as a whole and is being provided in the form of overall or sector budget support. Governments then have more flexibility in how they allocate their own budget to education. However, in a situation of economic or financial hardship, aid to higher education is likely to be competing with other priorities such as poverty alleviation, food subsidies, or energy.

Main Features of Current Funding Policies and Practices

In most countries, budgetary practices remain largely traditional. University operating budgets use the previous year(s) as a baseline and make incremental changes based on general considerations such as the country's economic performance, government revenues, inflation rates, or institutional growth. Thus, in spite of the magnitude of financial needs confronting the institutions, their leeway, when considering a significant adjustment to their allocated amount, is minimal. Consequently, budget discussions are limited to fine-tuning the internal distribution of these fixed allocations among staff salaries, student services, staff development, and operational expenses. There are, in addition, other problems in budget management, such as the lack of transparency in decision-making, fragmentation in budget responsibilities and the absence of measures for curbing out-of-control budgets in higher education.

The inefficient application of funds often dilutes the impact of funds provided. This is the consequence of numerous factors, including the absence of defined funding mechanisms, poor system planning, poor monitoring of expenditures, excessive public expenditure on students studying overseas and inefficient use of available funds by higher education institutions, as demonstrated by high student dropout and repetition rates, high proportions of overhead and salary expenses for administrative staff, and high levels of institutional debt.

Some countries, however, have adopted more innovative budgetary practices and are beginning to move away from historically based budgets. Formulas can be based on cost per student, as in Kenya and Rwanda. Other countries, such as Nigeria and Ghana, use normative unit costs derived from prescribed student-teacher ratios by discipline and the recommended cost of goods and services for a teaching unit by discipline. For investment, some countries, such as South Africa, implement funding contracts linked to teaching and research outputs specified in government-approved plans. Various governments, such as Ethiopia, Ghana, Mozambique, and South Africa, supplement the core budgets of universities with competitive funds to stimulate qualitative improvements, research, and partnerships.

Faced with inadequate public financing, the share of private resources in higher education financing is expanding. The contribution from households accounts for approximately one-quarter of national expenditure (state and households) on higher education. It varies widely according to country, ranging from less than 10 percent in Mali, Chad, and the Republic of Congo to more than 50 percent in Uganda and Guinea-Bissau. However, household financing of higher education is relatively low when compared to household investment in other levels of education (30 percent of national expenditure in primary education and more than 45 percent in lower secondary education). This situation is peculiar to Africa and contributes to inequality in the education system, with the introduction of selection based on family resources well before a student's entry into higher education.

Different forms of cost sharing are being implemented in most African countries. As of 2009, at least 26 countries in Africa charge either tuition fees or other types of fees such as examination fees, registration fees, identity card fees, library fees, and management information system fees. Overall, higher education institutions in Africa generate about 30 percent of their income (from less than 5 percent in Madagascar and Zimbabwe to 56 percent in Uganda and 75 percent in Guinea-Bissau). Some countries, like Uganda, are implementing dual-track tuition policies whereby a certain number of free (or very low-cost) university places are awarded based on criteria such as academic excellence, income level, or positive discrimination, while other places are available on a tuition fee–paying basis or deferred-tuition policy. Even in some Francophone countries, such as Benin, where free higher education had long been considered a right, some public universities have chosen to charge fees for professional programs or programs of excellence.

To combine financial efficiency and equity goals, the introduction of tuition fees is accompanied by the development of financial aid programs and student loans. Financial assistance policies are critical components of cost-sharing policies in Africa. Most Francophone countries have privileged nearly universal financial assistance through free or subsidized social services (food, transportation, and housing) and scholarships for living expenses. Some have improved the targeting of public assistance and adopted means-tested policies. Student loans are operating in at least 13 African countries, mainly in Anglophone ones.

Cost recovery remains the main challenge in most countries for student loans to be effective and sustainable. The main issues facing student loans stem from interest rates that are set far too low, grace periods and repayment periods that are unnecessarily long and exacerbate the losses, and loans that are implemented in such a way that students are frequently unaware that they are incurring a real repayment obligation. In addition, legal systems often make debt collection expensive, and record keeping cannot adequately keep track of students or graduates. Finally, insufficient numbers of jobs in African economies challenge the ability of university graduates to repay their loans.

Private higher education has experienced spectacular growth in Africa and in 2006 accounted for 22 percent of higher education students, which is close to levels observed in Europe (28 percent on average), but below levels in Latin America (approximately 50 percent). This expansion has sought to address excess social demand and in a number of cases poor enrollment capacity and the issue of quality in the public sector. However, private higher education institutions also seek to provide educational programs that differ from those available in the public sector by offering short vocational programs in disciplines requiring limited technological investment in a bid to keep prices affordable. Their appeal largely depends on their ability to adapt and respond to labor market needs, thereby enhancing student employability.

Tools for Financially Sustainable Policies

Only a comprehensive approach that combines different tools can provide immediate as well as mid- and long-term solutions to ensure financial sustainability and thus preserve the quality of African higher education systems. Depending on the situation and constraints specific to each country, a number of measures will be more relevant or realistic than others. These measures include introducing cost sharing and more cost-efficient modes of delivery, managing student flows, streamlining social expenditure, improving governance and management practices, and providing incentives for private sector development. Solutions for the sustainable financing of higher education systems therefore exist provided a strategic medium-term approach for reform of the subsector is developed and backed by sustained political will and adequate and sustainable resources.

African governments ought to consider the adoption of performance-based budget allocations in place of historically determined allocations. Doing so would create a mechanism for correcting major institutional imbalances that have developed through the years and also inject greater transparency into the process, which would respond in part to growing demands for greater accountability in the use of public and private financing. In addition, performance-based allocations would encourage institutional autonomy as institutions must function under full management control if they are to be judged on the basis of their performance. In general, the improved use of public resources presupposes the existence of a reliable and efficient information, monitoring, and evaluation system and of teams trained in the use of these tools. Moreover, there are numerous possibilities for enhancing the effectiveness of available resources. Of these, improved management and the allocation of teaching and administrative staff based on needs, as well as the more systematic use of part-time and contract-based employment could have a profound impact on expenditure control. Other possibilities could include restructuring the educational program in the context, for example, of the Bologna process (LMD—*licence-master-doctorat*) initiated in several Francophone African countries.

The growth of the student population should be strategically managed. Failure to control student flow would lead to training young people who lack the relevant skills to benefit from the training or to investing in and encouraging studies that will result in more unemployment or underemployment. The selection can be considered upstream, at the secondary level, upon entry into higher education, or between the different tertiary cycles (especially between the *licence* and *master* degrees). Reducing the time necessary for students to graduate would help to slow down the increase in enrollment. The average duration of study is longer than necessary—due to a lack of regulation of enrollment or reenrollment, criteria for awarding scholarships or providing services to students that have no bearing on their academic performance, the frequent and unlimited retaking of classes, or even repeated changes of discipline. Simulations conducted in several countries reveal that the measures designed to select students based on ability and reduce the average duration of courses of study may have a considerable impact on the trend in the number of higher education students.

Cost sharing needs to be increasingly incorporated into funding strategies for the tertiary education sector and be accompanied by targeted scholarships or loans in order to maintain or even enhance accessibility for students from poor families. Effective student loan programs are possible in Sub-Saharan Africa, but they require both proper design and good execution. Student loans in Africa must be accompanied by other forms of financial assistance, including a judicious use of grants, especially where there is genuine evidence of aversion to student debt, as well as repayment forbearance and eventual forgiveness in cases of lifetime low incomes or other conditions that contribute to unmanageable repayment burdens.

Scholarships and other forms of student financial aid need to be better targeted and rationalized to better meet the goals of equity and efficiency. In many countries, grant and scholarship allocation criteria are linked to academic performance rather than to university places, socioeconomic disadvantage, or priority disciplines for the country's development. Without revised legislation, there is the risk that the system will accumulate yearly cost overruns and that grants will take up even more of the higher education budget, not to mention inequity and inefficiency issues that will arise as a result of lacking or weak targeting of assistance aid.

Scholarships for studies abroad, accounting for a significant share of the higher education budget (on average, 18 percent in Africa) are usually allocated to beneficiaries from the most privileged social groups, and the criteria for the award of these scholarships often lack transparency. If the number of these scholarships were strictly limited to fields that are especially relevant to national development, a portion of these resources could be set aside for the provision of quality local educational programs.

Public-private partnerships can improve the efficiency of services provided to students—such as meals, housing, and transportation. In most cases, these services are not provided exclusively to the neediest students and are becoming financially unsustainable as a result of the increase in student numbers. Establishing a public-private partnership through which the state would delegate the provision of these services to private entrepreneurs would help to reduce the cost of these services without penalizing the students. The state would play the role of facilitator and regulator (definition of approved housing standards and costs, incentives, monitoring, and control), particularly by requiring that costs be affordable for students. In return, the state would offer tax or other incentives (land, provision of services, development of common areas, various types of assistance, low-interest loans, assumption of a portion of rental costs with a view to providing a subsidized rental rate, and so forth), thus attracting developers and securing a return on investments. Such a partnership would ensure that public expenditure is allocated as a priority to academic activities and research and not to the provision of services to students.

The diversification of financing requires that higher education institutions be able to generate their own resources. These resources could be derived from services pertaining to specific vocational training, continuing training programs (degree and nondegree), or expert or research services. Numerous examples exist in Africa. To develop income-generating activities, higher education institutions must enjoy sufficient autonomy in order to be able to manage their budget in accordance with their development objectives. They must also ensure genuine transparency in the redistribution of generated resources.

The private sector can help to diversify the provision of education and absorb a percentage of the increase in the number of students if it is appropriately staffed to provide quality. Governments should focus public financing on educational programs in the sectors where there is inadequate provision and in those of national strategic importance and should promote access by disadvantaged students. In order to ensure that the private sector supplements the public educational program, it is necessary to develop a regulatory framework that stipulates in particular the requirements for the establishment of institutions and programs, the accreditation of degrees and teachers, and the criteria for evaluation. In some cases, it may prove useful to encourage private developers to invest in higher education through tax measures (a more attractive tax system for institutions recognized as serving the public interest, reduced customs duties) or other measures (provision of land or buildings, access to loans) as well as in the national accreditation of degrees.

The Implementation of Financing Reforms

Financing reforms are difficult, and some prerequisites are necessary for their successful implementation. Social assessment of the proposed reforms through wide consultation is necessary to build consensus among the diverse constituents of the tertiary education community, while allowing for a high degree of tolerance for controversies and disagreements. The purpose is to make all stakeholders aware of the linkage between the proposed reforms and the likely improvements in teaching and learning conditions these could bring about. Additional resources can be mobilized and channeled toward tertiary education institutions and other concerned groups, such as students, to facilitate the acceptance of reforms that challenge the status quo. This can help to transform what could be called an "undoing reform" into a "constructing" reform. Another way to increase political acceptability and avoid disruptions is to introduce "grandfather" provisions and transitory funding arrangements that guarantee, for all institutions and beneficiary groups, amounts of resources equal to those they would have received under the previous system, at least for some period of time. Similarly, in order to reduce resistance to change, financing reforms can only be implemented with new institutions rather than existing universities. Finally, thinking about the timing and proper sequencing of reforms is very important.

The ability to implement significant changes in resource mobilization, allocation, and utilization depends on the existence of favorable governance arrangements. This implies granting increased management autonomy to public tertiary education institutions. In return, performance objectives, accountability and reporting channels, should be clearly defined. This performance can be monitored through the evaluation-accreditation system in countries where one exists. Modifying the mode of appointment of university leaders and the role and configuration of university boards can also be used to accompany financing reforms. To enact the new financing policies, governments and tertiary institutions should implement effective strategic planning at the national and institutional levels and modern financial management procedures. They should rely on analytical techniques to predict the direction and magnitude of the consequences of reforms. This would enable them to identify problems early on and make the necessary adjustments thanks to adequate monitoring systems. Finally, they could protect financing reforms from political interference by strengthening the regulatory framework and institutional structure.

Purpose and Organization of the Study

This study seeks to call the attention of governments and the international community to the difficulties of securing financing for higher education in Africa and the urgent need to modify policies. Difficulties in financing higher education are universal, but their magnitude and consequences in Africa are singular: (a) growth in demand is extremely high, (b) the fiscal base is very weak, (c) public spending per student is declining, (d) primary education is not yet universal and remains a priority, and (e) families' contributions are relatively larger in primary education than in higher education.

The study also aims to address the information deficit regarding financing practices, resource origin, allocation modalities, and resource use in higher education in Africa. Although most countries have difficulties related to financing and budgetary practices often remain traditional, certain governments and institutions have taken measures to address these challenges, utilizing financing formulas that allow for resource diversification, favor optimal resource allocation, or lead to efficiency gains. By shedding light on various financing practices, this study hopes to encourage more transparency and better resource management to increase actors' responsibility for results.

Finally, the suggestions offered by this study are based on African experiences in reforming higher education financing. Policy tools for controlling student numbers, mobilizing private resources, reducing costs, and improving management can provide a credible response to the financing crisis. This work calls on governments and institutions to equip themselves with the indicators and management tools that will allow them to gain control of their expenses and to orient higher education policy toward their countries' development needs. The study takes the majority of its examples from Africa in order to show that this possibility exists and that governments should rely first and foremost on themselves in developing appropriate solutions. Thus an exchange of experience regarding financing practice can begin.

This study consists of five chapters. Chapter 2 describes the demand for higher education, its projected evolution from now until 2015, and countries' capacity to respond to the associated financing needs. Chapter 3 describes the financing policies and practices currently in use in African countries. Chapter 4 proposes tools to improve higher education financing, and chapter 5 discusses how to ensure that financing reforms are implemented.

CHAPTER 2

Rising Social Demand and the Challenge of Sustainable Financing

The level of public investment in higher education in Africa has remained steady over the past 15 years, with the continent allocating an estimated 0.78 percent of its gross domestic product (GDP) to higher education. Although higher than the average rate of non-African developing countries (0.66 percent), this share falls short of the average for the Organisation for Economic Co-operation and Development (OECD) countries (1.21 percent). Furthermore, in the poorest African countries, the share dips to 0.63 percent, largely as a result of their limited tax base (see table 2.1).

Overall, in the past 15 years, African countries have maintained their commitment to higher education. Africa allocates approximately 20 percent of its current public expenditure on education to the higher education subsector (see table 2.2). This rate is comparable to the world average and higher than the corresponding rate of non-African developing countries (18 percent).

As figure 2.1 indicates, however, the priority given to higher education in the context of overall public expenditure on education varies considerably from country to country. These differences are due to specific circumstances or political choice rather than to disparities in wealth among countries, differences between the English- or French-speaking countries, the relative size of the private higher education sector, or even the level of development of the education sector.

Table 2.1 Public Expenditure on Higher Education as a Percentage of GDP, by Country Group, 1990 and 2006

Country group	1990		2006 (or closest year)	
	Expenditure as percentage of GDP	Number of countries	Expenditure as percentage of GDP	Number of countries
Africa	0.75	38	0.78	49
Low-income	0.67	25	0.63	32
Other	0.91	13	1.06	17
OECD	—	—	1.21	27
Non-African developing countries	0.56	33	0.66	36
World	0.69	85	0.84	146

Sources: Authors' calculations based on national, UNESCO Institute for Statistics (UIS), and World Bank data.
Note: — = not available.

Table 2.2 Share of Higher Education in Current Public Expenditure on Education, by Country Group, 1990 and 2006

Country group	1990		2006 (or closest year)	
	Higher education as percentage of public expenditures on education	Number of countries	Higher education as percentage of public expenditures on education	Number of countries
Africa	21.2	39	20.0	49
Low-income	21.8	26	20.0	32
Other	20.2	13	20.1	17
OECD	—	—	23.4	27
Non-African developing countries	16.3	35	17.6	38
World	18.6	89	19.8	150

Sources: Authors' calculations based on national, UIS, and World Bank data.
Note: — = not available.

In countries that are far from ensuring universal school enrollment at the primary level, a balanced and fair education policy would recommend prioritizing that level and channeling a smaller share of public resources to postprimary education. This would apply particularly to higher education, which sits at the top of the education pyramid. However, this logic has not been applied in many countries, including Burkina Faso, Burundi, Côte d'Ivoire, Ethiopia, Malawi, the Central African Republic, Rwanda, and Chad, where higher education absorbs more than 20 percent of the

Figure 2.1 Share of Higher Education in Current Public Expenditure on Education in African Countries, 2006 (or Closest Year)

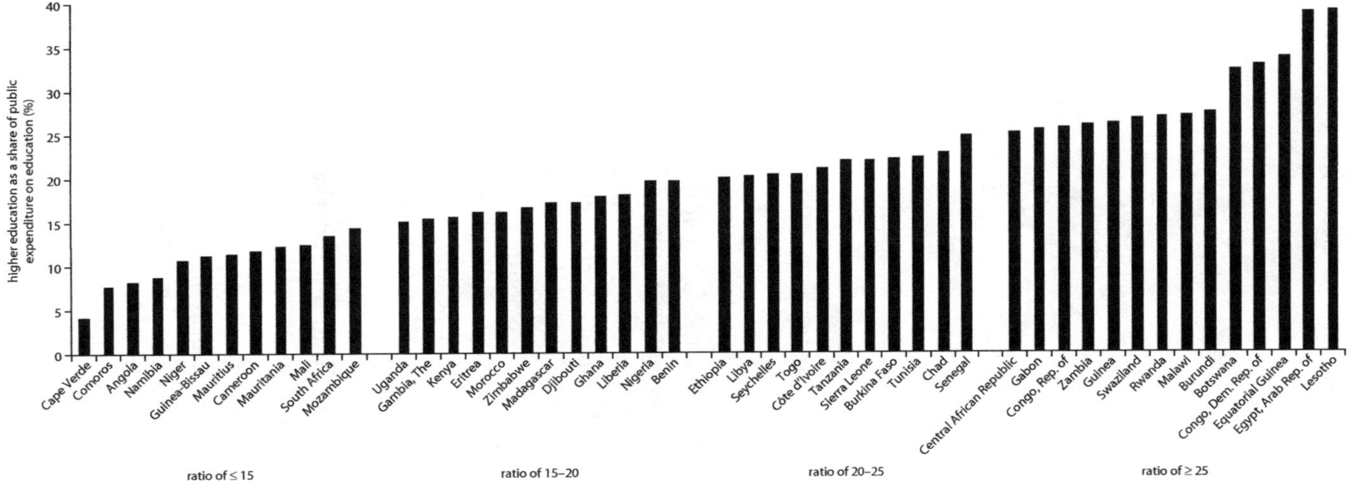

Sources: Authors' calculations based on national, UIS, and World Bank data.

Figure 2.2 Public Expenditure on Higher Education and the Form of the Education Pyramid in African Countries, 2006 (or Closest Year)

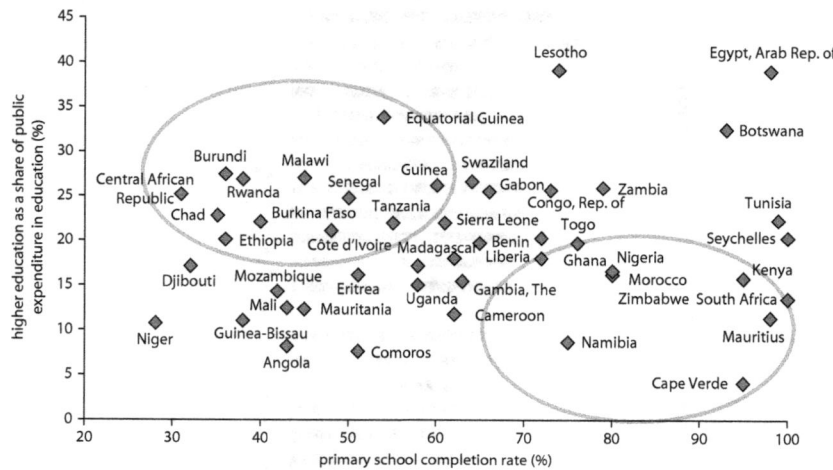

Sources: Authors' calculations based on national data, UIS, World Bank, and country sector study data. UNESCO, BREDA 2007 for the completion rates.

education budget despite the fact that the primary education completion rate is less than 50 percent (see figure 2.2).[1]

Conversely, countries that have attained—or are on the verge of attaining—universal primary school enrollment would be expected to allocate a larger share of their education budget to higher education. Yet in some countries such as South Africa, Cape Verde, Ghana, Kenya, Morocco, Mauritius, and Namibia, where at least 70 percent of each age cohort completes primary school, higher education absorbs less than 20 percent of public education resources.

Current Demand for Higher Education and Government Funding Capacity

The problem of higher education financing is more acute in Africa than in the rest of the world. In the last 15 years, the total number of higher education students in Africa has tripled, increasing from 2.7 million in 1991 to 9.3 million in 2006 (an average annual rate of 16 percent), while public resources allocated to current expenditure in that sector have only doubled (increasing at an average annual rate of 6 percent). Accordingly, the mean ratio between the average increase in the number of students and the increase in resources between 1991 and 2006 is 1.45 (see table 2.3). In the rest of the world, public financing of higher education has in general kept pace with the increase in the number of higher education students. The situation is even more critical in the poorest African countries where, in the period 1991–2006, the number of students quadrupled, while the available public resources increased at most 75 percent.

The challenges facing higher education financing in Africa are particularly severe because of the continent's rate of population growth. The achievement of universal primary education by 2020 would imply on average a 240 percent increase in the number of primary school students (Ledoux 2007). Moreover, to maintain the current rate of transition from primary to lower secondary education, the number of students would have to increase by a factor of 2.5 by 2020 (an achievement feasible for 10 countries, but difficult or very difficult for 21 other countries). Furthermore, some countries' commitment to ensuring 9 to 10 years of basic education for all young people implies a 420 percent increase in the number of lower secondary education students (which seems feasible within the time limit envisaged for 5 countries, but difficult—or impossible—for 26 other countries). The financial implications of these projections are significant (see figure 2.3). Assuming that African countries allocate 20 percent of their national resources to the education sector,

Table 2.3 Ratio between the Increase in the Number of Higher Education Students and the Increase in Public Resources Allocated to Current Expenditure on Higher Education, by Country Group, 1991 and 2006

Country group	Number of countries in group	Number of students in 2006 as a multiple of the 1991 level (A)	Aggregate current expenditure on higher education in 2006 as a multiple of the 1991 level (B)	Ratio (A/B)
Africa	36	2.84	1.96	1.45
Low-income	23	4.32	1.73	2.50
Other	13	2.61	2.18	1.20
Non-African developing countries	18	3.34	3.19	1.04

Sources: Authors' calculations based on national, UIS, and World Bank data.
Note: The analysis is limited to 36 African and 18 non-African countries, the only countries for which data since 1991 are available on both the number of higher education students and the public resources allocated to higher education (expressed here in constant 2000 U.S. dollars).

Figure 2.3 Change in the Number of Higher Education Students and Expenditure on Higher Education in Two Groups of African Countries, 1991–2006

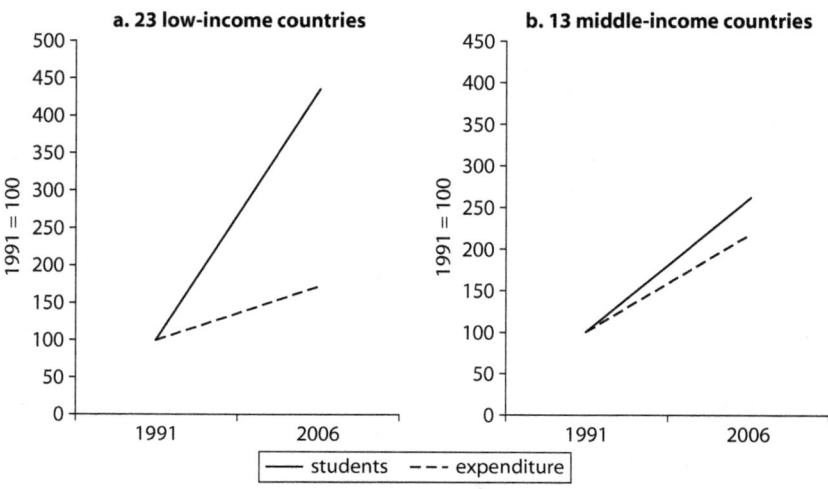

Sources: Authors' calculations based on national, UIS, World Bank, and country sector study data.

they will have to seek international financing equivalent to 150 percent of national funds if they are to respond to quantitative development while ensuring a level of quality considered "favorable" or at least "acceptable." This would imply reaching an estimated 60 percent rate of dependence on external assistance.[2]

As figure 2.4 illustrates, the situation varies from country to country. In some countries such as Botswana, Ethiopia, Lesotho, Madagascar, Malawi, Morocco, Sierra Leone, Swaziland, and Zambia (countries with a ratio close to 1), the amount of public resources allocated to higher education has kept pace with the number of students. However, in countries such as Burkina Faso, Cameroon, Côte d'Ivoire, The Arab Republic of Egypt, Guinea, Kenya, Mali, Mauritius, and Togo (countries with a ratio above 3), this has clearly not been the case.

The issue of higher education financing must be considered in the context of the development of the education sector. Within the education budget, allocations to each subsector involve trade-offs with the others. Moreover, the increase in the number of higher education students is directly related to progress achieved in the area of universal primary school enrollment and secondary school enrollment. Thus, the quantitative and qualitative enhancement of higher education should not be viewed in isolation but must be considered in the context of a

Figure 2.4 Ratio between the Change in the Number of Higher Education Students and the Amount of Public Resources Allocated to Current Expenditure on Higher Education in African Countries, 1991–2006

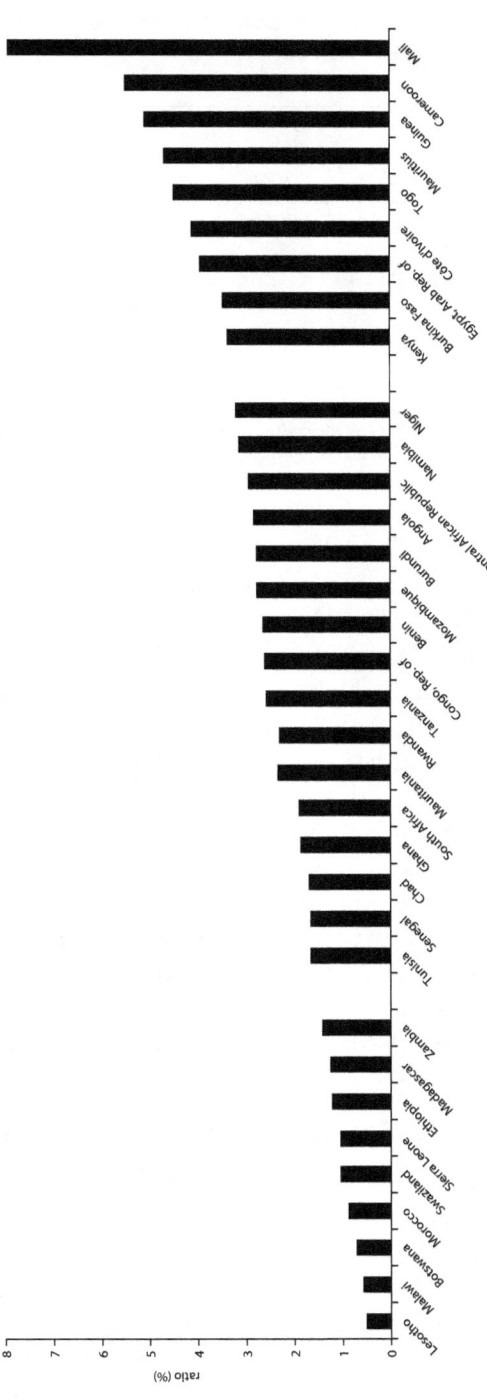

Sources: Authors' calculations based on national, UIS, and World Bank data.
Note: A ratio value above 1 indicates an increase in the number of higher education students greater than the increase in public resources allocated to current expenditure on higher education.

Table 2.4 Average Gross Enrollment Ratio in 31 Sub-Saharan African Countries, by Level of Education, 1990–2005
% unless otherwise noted

Level of education	1990	1999	2005	Average annual change, 1990–2005
Primary education	67.8	75.7	92.5	2.1
Lower secondary education	18.7	25.4	35.0	4.3
Upper secondary education	8.6	11.7	15.8	4.1
Higher education (number of students per 100,000 inhabitants)	160.0	245.0	291.0	4.1

Source: Mingat, Ledoux, and Rakotomalala 2009.
Note: Benin, Burkina Faso, Cameroon, the Central African Republic, Chad, the Republic of Congo, Côte d'Ivoire, the Democratic Republic of Congo, Eritrea, Ethiopia, The Gambia, Ghana, Guinea-Bissau, Kenya, Lesotho, Madagascar, Malawi, Mali, Mauritania, Mozambique, Niger, Nigeria, Rwanda, Senegal, Sierra Leone, Sudan, Tanzania, Togo, Uganda, Zambia, and Zimbabwe.

coordinated and consistent development of the education sector. The potential to develop higher education depends on choices made as part of flow management (policies to manage enrollment) and financial trade-offs at each education level within the framework of limited resources.

In the last 15 years, the education sector in Sub-Saharan Africa has grown significantly and has made steady progress in school enrollment (see table 2.4). However, the number of students at all education levels has increased faster than public resources have been made available. This is true not only for higher education but also for other education levels, where public expenditure per student has declined.

The decline in public expenditure per student and projected increase in population suggest the need for a systemic approach that addresses the issue of higher education quality in conjunction with a flow management policy at secondary and primary education levels (see UNESCO, BREDA 2007).

Public Resources per Student and Efforts to Raise Quality

Africa is the only region in the world that has experienced a decrease in the volume of current public expenditure per student (by 30 percent in the last 15 years; see table 2.5). Nonetheless, Africa's current average annual public expenditure per student remains relatively high (amounting to approximately US$2,000 in 2006) and is more than double the respective average for non-African developing countries (see table 2.6). Although the amount in question is five times lower than the OECD

Table 2.5 Average Public Expenditure per Student in 18 Sub-Saharan African Countries, by Level of Education, 1975, 1990, and 2003

Level of education	Public expenditure per student as percentage of GDP per capita			Average annual change (%)	
	1975	1990	2003	1975–90	1990–2003
Primary education	0.20	0.15	0.12	−2.00	−1.80
Secondary education	1.21	0.61	0.47	−4.50	−2.00
Higher education	12.22	7.32	4.29	−3.40	−4.00

Sources: For the period 1975–90, Mingat and Suchaut 2000; for 2003, Mingat, Ledoux, and Rakotomalala 2009.

Table 2.6 Annual Public Expenditure per Student, by Country Group, 1990 and 2006

Country group	Expenditure per student (2006 US$)		Expenditure per student as percentage of GDP per capita	
	1990	2006	1990	2006
Africa	2,900	2,000	352.7	292.7
Low-income	1,800	1,330	459.6	356.1
Other	2,800	3,200	228.1	170.3
OECD	9,700	11,500	38.9	31.8
Non-African developing countries	460	875	63.4	63.2
World	2,550	4,600	130.7	124.4

Source: Authors' calculations based on country sector data as well as UIS, United Nations, and World Bank data.

average and less than half the world average (see table 2.6), factoring in the gap in the standard of living sheds a different light on the issue: the ratio of annual public expenditure per student to GDP per capita is approximately 3.0 in Africa, but only 0.3 in OECD countries and 1.2 at the global level. These comparisons suggest the presence of Africa-specific cost drivers (Brossard and Foko 2008). One reason for the high cost is social spending (see chapter 3). There is, however, a highly variable level of public spending per student across African countries (from a factor of 1 to a factor of 14 among 27 low-income African countries). This suggests that countries with the lowest levels of spending per student probably provide insufficient funding to assure services of a reasonable quality, while those with the highest levels probably have systems that are wasteful (Mingat, Ledoux, and Rakotomalala 2009).

Although the impact of this decline in public resources on the functioning of higher education varies considerably from country to country, it is probably more significant in countries that have a low rate of public expenditure per student and face a steep increase in the number of students. As figure 2.5 shows, the volume of recurrent public expenditure per student varies among African countries by factors ranging from 1 to more than 10. Higher-income countries tend to allocate more public resources per student, but that trend is not uniform. Broadly speaking, there are three categories of countries. At one extreme, approximately 15 countries spend less than US$1,000 per student (roughly half of the African average). At the other, there is a group of 13 countries including two particularly low-income economies—Malawi and Chad—whose expenditure per student exceeds the African average. One should be cautious when making this comparison since the structure of public expenditure per student differs from one country to another. Also, the relative importance of private funding for higher education institutions (either from households or from own generated revenues) may also differ from one country to another.

Juxtaposed, figures 2.4 and 2.5 demonstrate that, in recent years, public expenditure per student tends to be higher where the increase in the number of students has been moderate compared to the increase in public resources allocated to higher education. In other words, the financing situation is relatively favorable in countries such as Lesotho, Botswana, or Zambia, but critical in countries such as Mali, Burkina Faso, Guinea, Cameroon, and Togo (see figure 2.6).

Impact on Quality

Evidence shows that in countries with inadequate public financing and resource diversification, admitting increasing numbers of students results in a deterioration in quality.[3] Governments and institutions throughout Africa have implemented various policies designed to reduce costs, including freezing salaries and recruitment of teaching staff, reducing student social aid and scholarships, eliminating expenditure on books and equipment, and forgoing basic maintenance and repair activities. Without associated efficiency gains, these measures have had a negative impact on the quality of the higher education sector. Universities find it increasingly difficult to maintain adequate student-teacher ratios (see figure 2.7), lecture halls are overcrowded, buildings fall into disrepair, teaching equipment is not replaced, investment in research and in training new instructors is insufficient, and many lecturers are obliged to supplement their income by offering their services in the private sector. At worst, inadequate funding may lead to student protests and strikes, jeopardizing the completion of the academic year. Madagascar offers an instructive

Figure 2.5 Annual Current Public Expenditure per Student in African Countries, 2006 (or Closest Year)

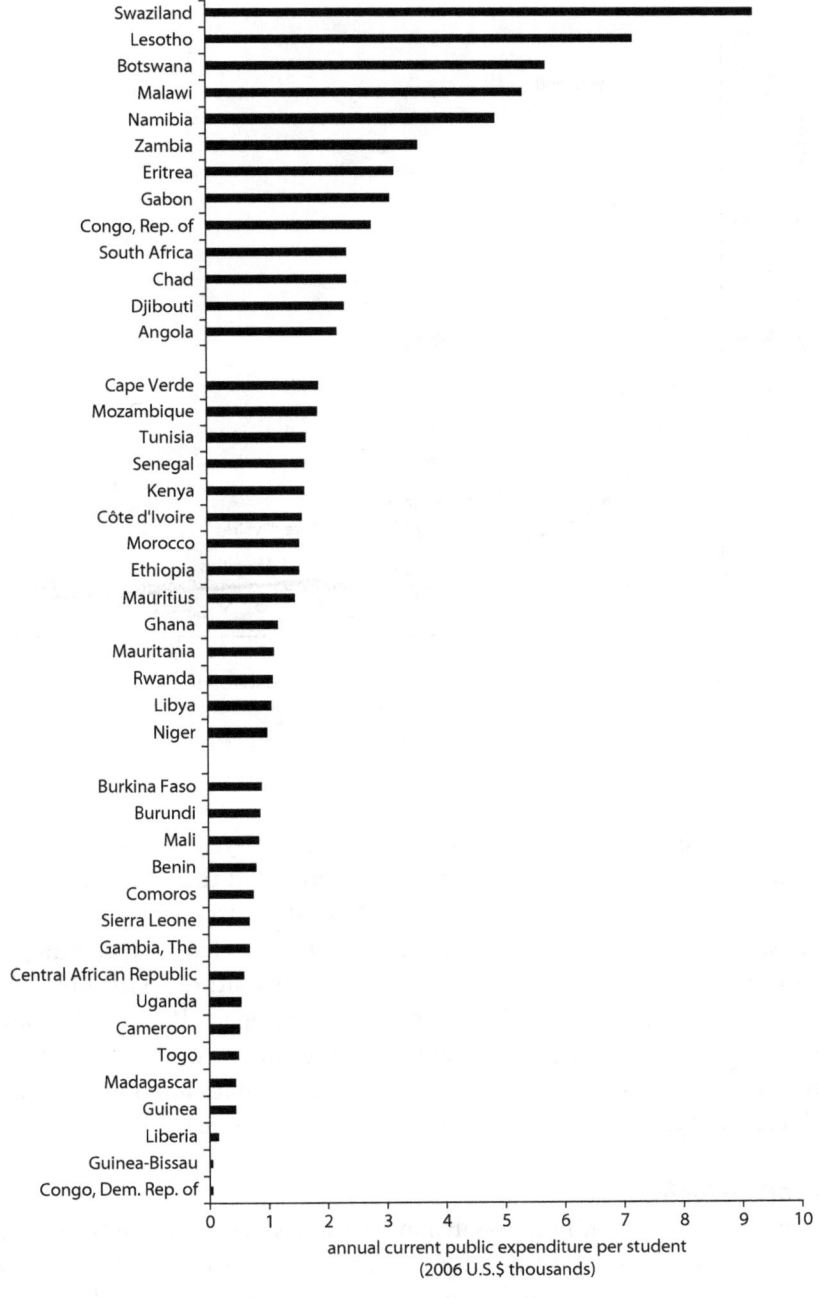

Sources: Authors' calculations based on national, UIS, World Bank, and country sector data.

Figure 2.6 Public Expenditure per Student and Ratio of the Number of Students to the Current Level of Public Expenditure on Higher Education in Select African Countries, 2006

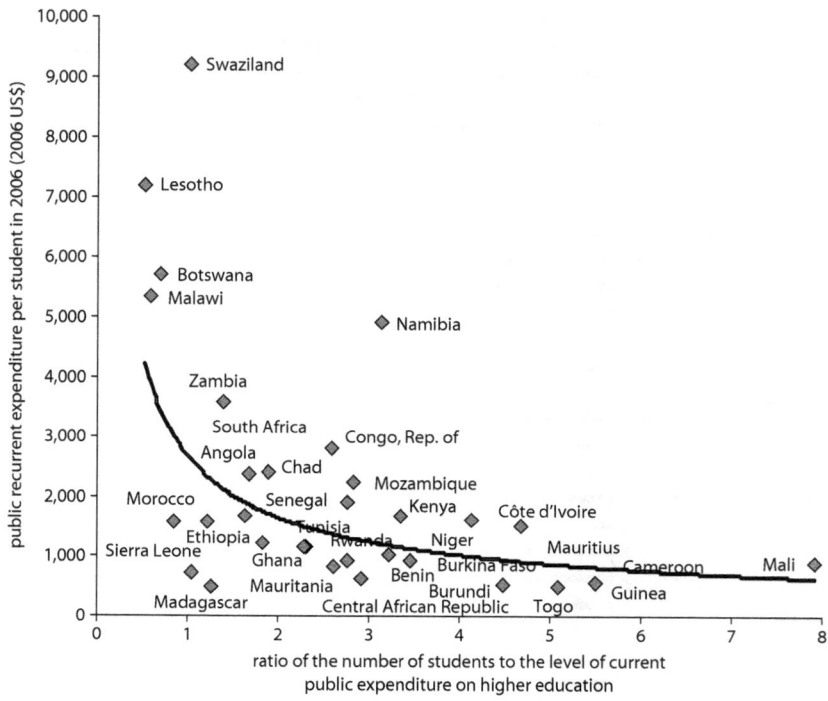

Sources: Authors' calculations based on national, UNESCO Institute of Statistics (UIS), World Bank, and country sector data.

example (see Salmi 2008). In that country, a 10-year freeze on hiring instructors has driven up student-teacher ratios and the teaching load of the remaining staff, many of whom work overtime to beef up their meager salaries. As a result, the average age of instructors has risen alarmingly: almost one-fourth of the faculty is over 60. Expenditure on maintenance has been sparse, and the infrastructure is falling apart. Reportedly, some regional universities experience power and telephone outages for several hours in a day because of unpaid utility bills. Supplies are often unavailable, and libraries have not purchased a textbook in years.

Funding for Research

Funding for research in Sub-Saharan Africa has declined significantly in recent decades as priorities have shifted toward sectors such as health care, basic education, and infrastructure development (World Bank 2008a).

Figure 2.7 Student-Teacher Ratio in Higher Education in Select African Countries, Public and Private Sectors Combined, 2006 (or Closest Year)

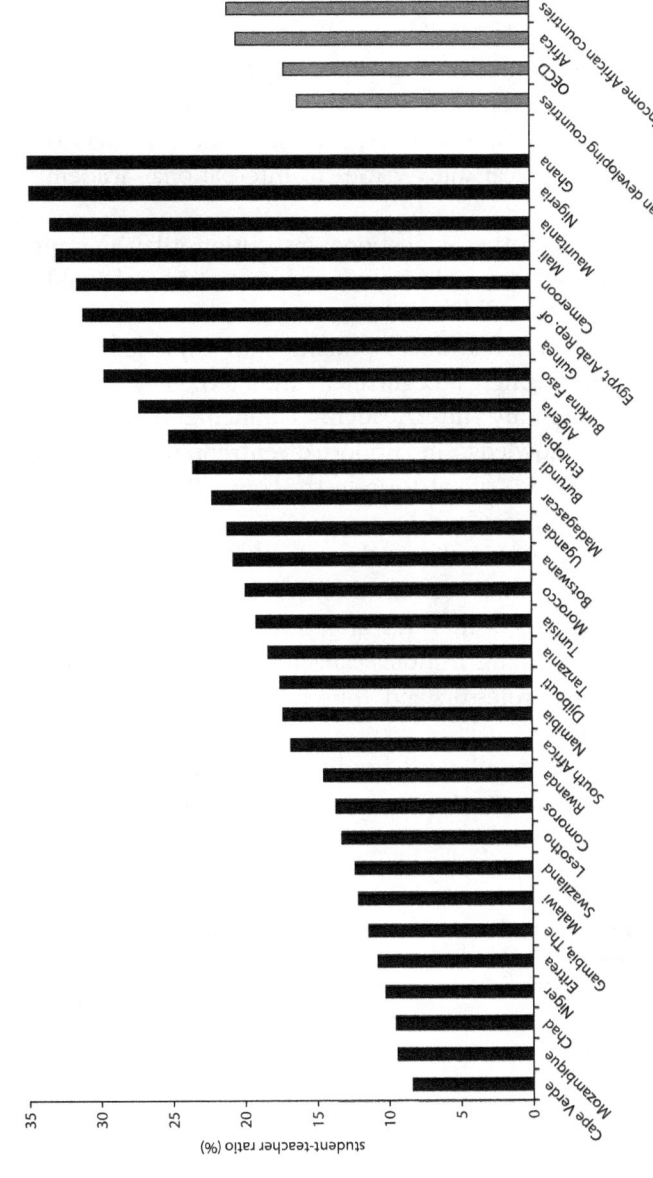

Sources: Pôle de Dakar 2008, based on UIS country-specific and OECD data.

Soaring enrollment and falling expenditures per student throughout the continent have also contributed to this decline in funding by favoring allocations to teaching instead of research and to undergraduate instead of postgraduate training.

The inadequacy of funding has limited institutions' ability to offer adequate remuneration or to invest in infrastructure, research facilities, and equipment, thereby hindering overall research capacity. The consequences of this situation are evident when one considers the minimal contribution of African universities to international academic research (see table 2.7).

Universities and other educational institutions play an important role as society's knowledge hubs, where concentrations of highly qualified senior faculty at the PhD level can engage in innovative research that contributes to national development. This knowledge and applied research are increasingly recognized as among the key sources of growth in the global economy (InterAcademy Council 2004). In particular, the application of knowledge in support of entrepreneurship and research and development is critical to industry competitiveness and economic growth.

Moreover, research quality and productivity have significant implications for educational institutions themselves, which are often judged by the level and quality of their research output. The resulting reputational impact will affect an institution's capacity to attract distinguished scholars and train new professors and, thus, ultimately the quality of its learning environment.

The repercussions of poor funding for PhD-level faculty and students will be even more dramatic in the future. Students will be unable to pursue further study because of the lack of funding mechanisms to

Table 2.7 Number of Scientific Publications and Patent Applications, by Region, 2002

Region	Scientific publications	Patent applications filed by residents
East Asia and Pacific	25,391	65,506
Europe and Central Asia	40,043	32,728
Latin America and the Caribbean	16,789	40,003
Middle East and North Africa	4,468	926
South Asia	12,127	2,143
Sub-Saharan Africa	3,696	101

Source: World Bank 2009.

support themselves and a lack of quality courses and teaching staff to maintain higher-level programs. Poor funding will consistently diminish the incentive for high-level faculty to remain in the academic or research field when other sectors are more profitable.[4] Thus, while social demand for access to higher education will continue to rise, the number of new academics joining the system will decline. Already, analysis shows that for about 10 countries in the region, the average percentage of highly educated staff (for example, PhD or master's level) in public higher education institutions is less than 20 percent. If the status quo persists, Sub-Saharan African countries will face a severe shortage of faculty at a time when high-level skills and research capacity are needed most.

Projected Demand for Higher Education and Public Financing

The increasing number of students completing primary school and wishing to continue their studies generates pressures on the higher education system that African countries are ill-prepared to address (UNESCO, BREDA 2007).[5]

This section builds on earlier studies and comprises three parts: first, an examination of the current quantitative expansion of higher education in Africa and, on the basis of the trends observed, an estimate of the future number of students; second, an analysis of the implications for public financing given the current forms of organization and provision of education services; and third, a discussion of the sustainability of current expansion rates at the physical and logistics levels, particularly with regard to building capacity and recruiting and training instructors.[6]

Trends in Enrollment

Demand for higher education has expanded significantly on the African continent as a whole, and African institutions have responded by admitting greater numbers of students each year. Between 2000 and 2006, the total number of students increased from 6.0 million to 9.3 million. This can be compared to the 1994–2000 period, in which 2.5 million new students registered. A projection of the recent trends in individual countries (taking into consideration the initial conditions prevailing there) suggests that the entire continent will have between 18 million and 20 million students by 2015 (see figure 2.8).[7]

Because the projection is based on the most recent expansion rates identified in the countries concerned, these numbers are likely to be

Figure 2.8 Change in the Number of Higher Education Students in Africa, 1982–2006 and Projected through 2015

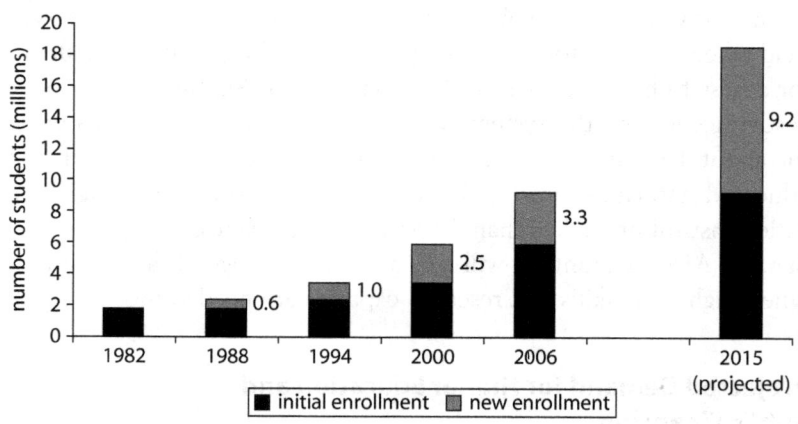

Sources: Authors' calculations based on national, UIS, and World Bank data.

attained.[8] In other words, by 2015 and at the current rate of expansion, the African continent is expected to have twice as many students as in 2006. This projection is conservative in that it underestimates the possible expansion of secondary education in conjunction with the strong demographic pressure that the continent is experiencing. As a result, the gross access rate at the end of upper secondary education in Africa has more than doubled since 1990, increasing from 9 percent in 1991 to 19 percent in 2005 (UNESCO, BREDA 2005, 2007).

As figure 2.9 indicates, the situation varies considerably from country to country. In approximately 10 countries, the number of students in higher education in 2015 will be at least triple the current level. In approximately 20 countries, the number of students is expected to increase by a factor of between 2 and 3, compared to the 2006 level. For the remaining group of approximately 20 countries, that factor is expected to be less than 2. In any case, the challenge of increasing numbers of students is often particularly relevant for countries in which the financing of their higher education systems deteriorated during the last decade (figure 2.4). The expected aggravation of the crisis in those countries calls for ambitious reforms.

Implications for Public Financing

In many African countries, the current rates of expansion will not be financially sustainable. The quest for sustainable development of the

Figure 2.9 Number of Students Expected in 2015 in African Countries on the Basis of Current Trends in Higher Education Growth

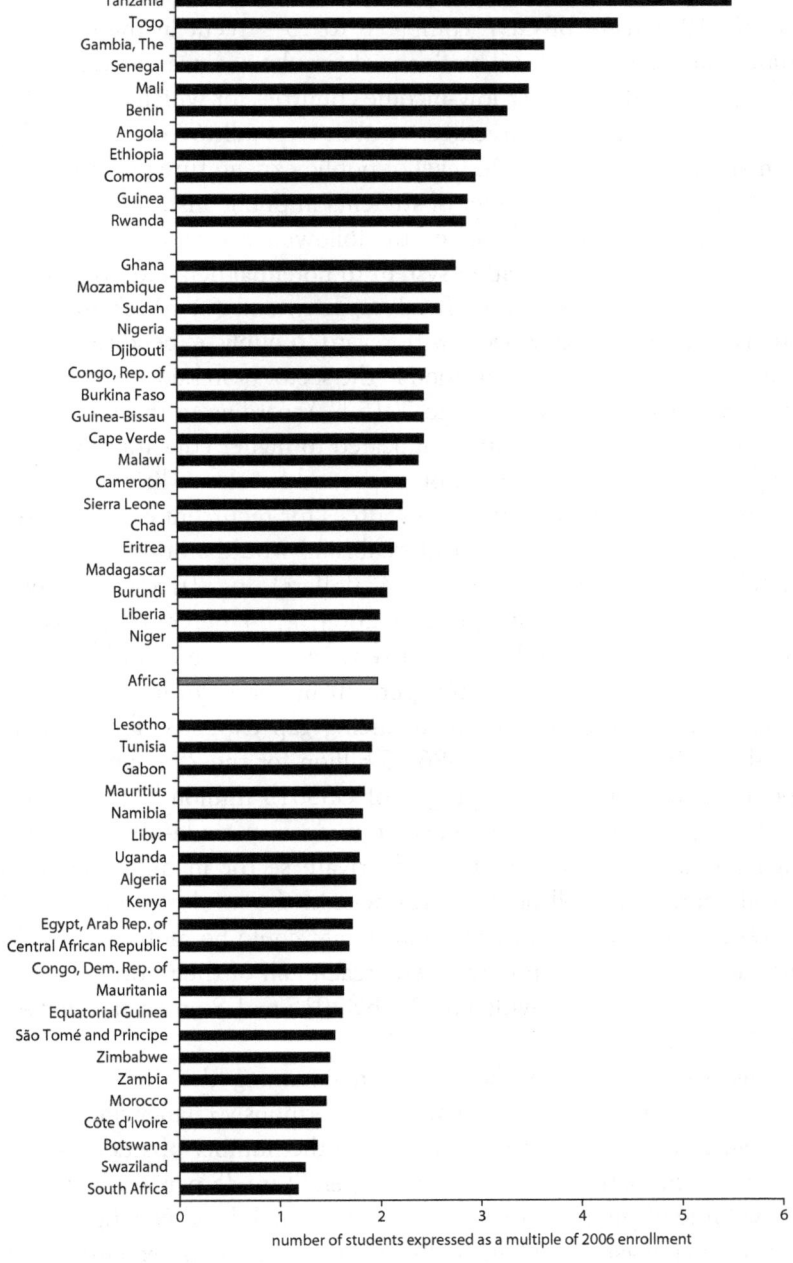

Sources: Authors' calculations based on national, UIS, and World Bank data.

higher education system is particularly critical in low-income African countries, whose narrower tax base translates into more limited public resources. On average, their public revenue in recent years has amounted to only 18 percent of GDP compared to 29 percent in the continent's middle-income countries. The financial simulations presented here have been developed for the 27 low-income countries for which data are available.[9] The simulations of recurrent public expenditure on higher education are based on the desired level of public expenditure per student and on the expected total number of students in public institutions.

The scenario tested is based on the following assumptions: (a) a favorable response of the education system to potential demand, (b) preservation of the countries' macro fiscal capacity, and (c) no change in the provision of education services with regard to public expenditure per student and share of private education in the sector or in budgetary trade-offs that favor higher education up to 2015.[10] According to this scenario, any increase in the public resources allocated to higher education will result solely from economic growth or improved fiscal conditions.[11] For the 27 countries as a whole, public resources for recurrent expenditure on higher education excluding studies abroad would amount to approximately US$914 million (in 2004 dollars) in 2015 compared to US$594 million actually spent in 2004, a 54 percent increase. On average, at the national level, recurrent expenditure would amount to US$2.19 billion in 2015, a 269 percent increase compared to 2004.

Accordingly, the cumulative financing gap expected for the period 2004–15 would amount to US$6.75 billion for the 27 countries, corresponding to an average annual gap of US$613 million.[12] This is only a "virtual" gap. Indeed, under current budgetary trade-offs in favor of higher education and the share of private sector in higher education enrollment, there will be an adjustment in the level of unit costs. The current expected amount of resources that could be mobilized suggests that unit costs should "progressively" reach half of their current level by 2015 (they should be divided by 2.4 by 2015 or 1.8 on average between 2005 and 2015).

This simple scenario shows that maintaining the current rates of expansion of higher education will be enormously challenging for most African countries. This sizable increase in the number of students would lead to a cumulative level of current expenditure 75 percent higher than the volume of public resources that may be mobilized (see figure 2.10). This financing gap would gradually widen at the rate of expansion of the systems themselves.

Figure 2.10 Current Expenditure on Higher Education and Public Expenditure Required to Expand Higher Education in Africa at Current Rates and Unit Costs, 2004–15

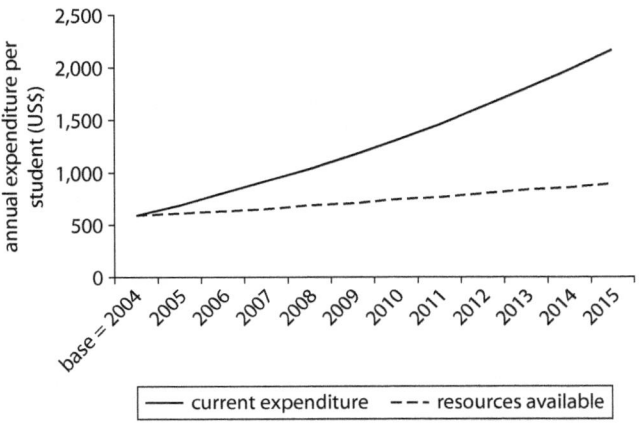

Sources: Authors' calculations based on national, UIS, United Nations, and World Bank data.
Note: This simulation concerns only 27 African countries.

The size of the financing gap suggests that alternative methods of financing and other models of expansion or organization of the supply of education services should be considered. In many countries, however, there will be little financing leeway. Higher education competes with other education levels for the appropriation of public resources, and even in countries where higher education enjoys a relatively high priority, the needs generated by progress toward universal primary school enrollment are expected to undermine that priority.

Although they take different forms in the various countries, the general findings shown in table 2.8 indicate that few countries can afford to maintain their current financing policies and rates of expansion. If the number of students is left unmanaged, available public resources per student are expected to decline further, to varying degrees depending on the country. This would result in a deterioration in the quality of services provided (the simulation avoids this by mandating consistent spending per student).

Human and Physical Constraints on Expansion

A sizable increase in the number of students would necessitate, among others, training a great number of qualified instructors, which would imply a considerable investment.

Table 2.8 Number of Students and Average Annual Expenditure Required to Support the Expansion of Higher Education in African Countries at Current Enrollment Rates and Unit Costs, 2004–15

	Total number of students			Average annual expenditure, 2004–15 (2004 US$ millions)[a]		
Country	2006	2015 trend value[a]	Ratio of 2015 to 2006	Resources	Expenditure	Difference (> 0 = gap)
Benin	58,560	192,700	3.3	27.6	66.3	39
Burkina Faso	30,472	75,200	2.5	23.1	37.8	15
Burundi	17,061	35,800	2.1	9.0	13.4	4
Central African Republic	9,673[a]	16,300	1.7	4.7	6.1	1
Chad	11,669[a]	25,100	2.2	9.2	13.2	4
Comoros	3,944[a]	10,800	3.0	1.2	3.5	2
Congo, Dem. Rep. of	223,372[a]	353,300	1.7	11.0	13.0	2
Côte d'Ivoire	135,221[a]	182,800	1.4	80.1	78.9	−1
Eritrea	5,474[a]	11,800	2.2	4.8	6.9	2
Ethiopia	180,286	544,100	3.0	107.6	197.8	90
Gambia, The	4,337	15,900	3.7	1.6	7.9	6
Guinea	42,711	123,800	2.9	27.9	77.9	50
Guinea-Bissau	4,624	11,400	2.5	0.1	1.1	1
Kenya	157,767	275,000	1.7	100.1	166.5	66
Madagascar	49,680	104,900	2.1	24.3	35.6	11
Malawi	7,121	17,200	2.4	16.9	33.0	16
Mali	45,635	159,500	3.5	20.9	47.6	27
Mauritania	13,021[a]	20,400	1.6	6.4	7.7	1
Mozambique	38,000	100,500	2.6	43.3	109.8	66
Niger	11,208	22,500	2.0	9.4	13.2	4
Rwanda	30,542[a]	85,800	2.9	33.6	67.8	34
Senegal	62,539	220,000	3.5	70.0	157.1	87
Sierra Leone	18,183[a]	40,700	2.2	8.7	16.1	7
Togo	28,371	124,400	4.4	10.9	29.4	18
Uganda	137,011	248,500	1.8	58.5	87.5	29
Zambia	33,592[a]	47,700	1.5	24.5	30.7	6
Zimbabwe	56,732[a]	96,700	1.5	75.7	98.6	23
Total, 27 countries	1,416,806	3,162,800	2.2	811.0	1,424.0	613
Cameroon	120,298	274,500	2.3	59.3	115.6	56
Congo, Rep. of	13,141	32,500	2.5	29.5	49.6	20
Lesotho	8,500	16,600	1.9	29.3	56.0	27
Total, 30 countries	1,558,745	3,486,400	2.2	929.0	1,645.0	716

Sources: Authors' calculations based on country sector data as well as UIS, United Nations, and World Bank data.
a. Authors' estimate.

If the current student-teacher ratio is to be maintained (20 students for one instructor), the number of instructors would have to increase from approximately 456,000 in 2006 to 908,000 in 2015.[13] If one takes into account retirements and other departures, estimated at 20 percent for the period 2006–15, it would be necessary to recruit and train approximately 566,000 new instructors over that period. In other words, every year it would be necessary to train 1.8 times more instructors than the annual number of instructors trained in the period 2000–06. In the case of Africa's approximately 30 low-income countries, roughly 270,000 new instructors would be required in the period 2006–15, which implies twice as many annual hirings as in the period 2000–06. Since in many countries the student-teacher ratio is hardly conducive to adequate instruction by international standards (figure 2.7), it is doubtful that the countries concerned would be able to recruit and train so many instructors even if the necessary financial resources were available.

However, it will be even harder for those countries to employ a sufficient number of senior faculty members (namely, professors and assistant professors), who are necessary for undertaking research, raising the scientific and pedagogical level of other instructors, and preparing future generations of instructors and research scientists. In fact, information available on approximately 10 countries in the region indicates that the proportion of senior faculty members is on average under 20 percent, in some cases considerably so (see table 2.9). In view of the low level of investment in research in Africa, it is doubtful that enough doctoral students can be trained to redress that situation.

Furthermore, the expansion of higher education systems will require considerable investment for increasing the capacity of existing establishments such as classrooms, libraries, laboratories, workshops, and lecture halls); setting up new facilities; ensuring a better geographic distribution; and improving the administrative and teaching equipment. In fact, the capacity of existing institutions in many countries is already largely insufficient. For instance, for every 100 student places theoretically available in public universities, the average number of students actually in attendance was 350 in Benin in 2007 (World Bank 2008b), 220 in Cameroon in 2006 (MINESUP 2007), and 260 in the Central African Republic in 2007 (Université de Bangui 2008). The classroom, library, and laboratory space available in Ugandan public universities was equivalent to 1.3 square meters per registered student (Uganda, Ministry of Education and Sports 2006). For comparison, the OECD ratio is 4–10 square meters.

Table 2.9 Proportion of Senior Faculty Members in Public Higher Education Institutions in Select African Countries

Country	Year	Percentage of faculty who are senior faculty members[a]	Percentage of lecturers with a master's degree or PhD
Algeria	2006	15	—
Benin	2007	17	—
Burkina Faso	2007	25	69
Cameroon	2006	16	—
Central African Republic	2006	35	—
Congo, Dem. Rep. of	2002	17	—
Congo, Rep. of	2005	10	—
Côte d'Ivoire	2007	18	—
Ethiopia	2003	—	9
Gabon	2002	12	—
Guinea	2006	16	28
Madagascar	1999	17	—
Rwanda[b]	2001	—	25
Tanzania	2006	18	52
Tunisia	2005	8	—
Uganda	2006	—	22
Average	n.a.	17.3	34.5

Source: Pôle de Dakar 2008.
Note: — = not available; n.a. = not applicable.
a. Professors and assistant professors.
b. National University of Rwanda only.

Based on the current rates of expansion of higher education, the overall investment and rehabilitation requirements are estimated at approximately US$45 billion (in 2006 dollars) for higher education in Africa as a whole, including US$20 billion for low-income countries.[14] (Investment requirements for the period 2006–15 have been assessed on the basis of a US$3,600, in 2006 dollars, cost estimate for 1 square meter per student, including the costs of service infrastructure, construction of teaching and administrative facilities, outfitting, and equipment.[15])

Assessments show that the capacity for public investment in higher education at the national level meets only 33–40 percent of total requirements in Africa as a whole (20–25 percent of the requirements of low-income countries).[16] This implies an investment financing deficit on the order of US$30 billion for the continent in the next 10 years, including US$15 billion for low-income countries alone. As a comparison, the financing deficit for those countries is 150 percent the size of the financing deficit implied by the capital expenditure necessary for universal primary school enrollment.[17]

Maintaining the quality of higher education requires a minimum level of resources below which the usefulness of the system should be called into question. In particular, if instructors are not remunerated in accordance with market standards (taking into account public budget constraints), the teaching profession will fail to attract instructors, and current faculty members will become demoralized and seek jobs on the side or move abroad. With significantly reduced public expenditure per student, it will become even more difficult to maintain existing equipment, buildings, and service infrastructure, which will exacerbate poor learning conditions and eventually generate social discontent. Yet for an effective contribution to the development of the continent, higher education in Africa must meet international standards of quality. Thus, African countries should adopt ambitious financing policies, which are detailed in chapter 4.

Notes

1. This rate is approximated by the gross rate of access to the last year of primary school.
2. A high rate (80 percent) of transition from primary to lower secondary education as a result of universal 9- to 10-year basic education and high rates of transition from lower to upper secondary education (65 percent) and from secondary to higher education.
3. By quality, we mean the inputs that are conducive to a good environment for training. At this level of analysis, it is impossible to assess the impact of a reduction in public expenditure per student on the quality of higher education. First, public expenditure per student is only part of the resources used and therefore constitutes only a partial and imperfect measure of higher education financing. Second, the use of resources should be studied to identify the expenditure items most affected. Third, there is not always a causal relationship between the level of expenditure and the quality of education.
4. In some African universities, the salaries of academic staff are about 20 percent of what they were 10 years earlier (ANSTI 2005).
5. The percentage of students finishing primary school and entering lower secondary education increased from 60 percent in 1990 to 80 percent in 2005.
6. This is based on studies carried out by the UNESCO, BREDA (2007) that, in the wake of other related publications, aim to provide updated factual information regarding higher education growth rates and their physical and financial implications with a view to enlightening national decision makers about

appropriate choices to be made in drawing up development policies for their education systems.

7. It is impossible to obtain detailed statistics for all African countries regarding transition from secondary to higher education and continuation at the higher education level. Accordingly, this simulation is based solely on the current rate of increase in the number of students and an assessment of potential additional demand created by the move toward universal primary school enrollment in individual countries. However, with regard to four countries (Benin, Burundi, Mali, and Mauritania) for which more detailed simulations are available (see Gioan 2007), findings based on current trends in upper secondary education (number of students registered for the last year and students who passed the school-leaving examination) and in higher education (among others, rates of admission and number of students leaving higher education) are relatively close. Even where they diverge as a result of different assumptions regarding the parameters used, the various projections suggest that demand for higher education will expand by 2015. In the case of Benin, for instance, the projected number of students by 2015 is approximately 193,000 by the first method compared to 200,000–245,000 by the second. In the case of Burundi, the respective figures are 36,000 compared to 31,000–39,000. In the case of Mali, they are approximately 160,000 compared to at most 112,000. And in the case of Mauritania, they are 21,000 compared to 21,000–39,000.

8. The projections presented here may be slightly at variance with those obtained by the same method in UNESCO, BREDA (2007). However, far from being incompatible, the two sets of projections are highly correlated (99 percent).

9. Namely, Benin, Burkina Faso, Burundi, the Central African Republic, Chad, the Comoros, Côte d'Ivoire, the Democratic Republic of Congo, Eritrea, Ethiopia, The Gambia, Guinea, Guinea-Bissau, Kenya, Madagascar, Malawi, Mali, Mauritania, Mozambique, Niger, Rwanda, Senegal, Sierra Leone, Togo, Uganda, Zambia, and Zimbabwe.

10. The base year chosen for the simulation is 2004, the most recent year for which the various higher education financing and operational parameters have been consolidated, ensuring adequate consistency of mobilized public resources with the current public expenditure actually observed.

11. The average GDP growth rate in 2004–15 has been set at 4 percent for all countries. Moreover, adopting the same approach as Bruns, Mingat, and Rakotomalala (2003) for simulating the costs of universal primary school enrollment, we have gradually increased the tax load in 2015 to 18 percent where it was initially between 14 and 18 percent, raised it to 14 percent where it was initially lower, and maintained it at its current level where it was initially higher than 18 percent.

12. Difference between simulated current expenditure and public resources over the period 2005–15.
13. This ratio is approximately equal to 20 and 17 students per instructor at the OECD and global levels, respectively. These figures suggest that instruction conditions in Africa are currently less satisfactory than average instruction conditions elsewhere in the world.
14. Consisting of 4 square meters per student by 2015; rehabilitation of 30 percent of initial installations (by upgrading the existing infrastructure and equipment) at a unit cost equal to 50 percent of full construction or equipment costs; and annual rehabilitation of 5 percent of all facilities under the same terms as initial rehabilitation. Total (initial and periodic) rehabilitation accounts for only 10 percent of cumulative investment requirements for the period 2006–15.
15. This estimate is based on experience in Côte d'Ivoire (see Gioan 2007).
16. Although the extent of investment requirements argues for allocating a considerable proportion of the higher education budget to investment in preparing the simulations, it is also necessary to reserve a reasonable part of that budget for current outlays, which are also important. A compromise is needed. Building on the current experience of OECD countries, we have opted for setting investment outlays at 10–12 percent of public expenditure on higher education with 2015 as a time horizon.
17. Bruns, Mingat, and Rakotomalala (2003) estimate the financing deficit resulting over the period 2001–15 from capital outlays necessary to achieve universal primary school enrollment in Africa by 2015 at approximately US$11 billion (in 2000 dollars or US$16 billion in 2006 dollars). In the absence of detailed data on the annual financing deficit, we have applied a simple proportionality rule. Accordingly, we have assumed that the cumulative deficit over the period 2007–15 would amount to US$10 billion (in 2006 dollars). That figure may then be compared to the US$15 billion estimate for higher education.

References

ANSTI (African Network of Scientific and Technological Institutions). 2005. *State of Science and Technology Training Institutions in Africa*. Nairobi: UNESCO.

Brossard, Mathieu, and Borel Foko. 2008. *Costs and Financing of Higher Education in Francophone Africa*. Africa Human Development Series. Washington, DC: World Bank.

Bruns, Barbara, Alain Mingat, and Ramahatra Rakotomalala. 2003. *Achieving Universal Primary Education by 2015: A Chance for Every Child*. Washington, DC: World Bank.

Gioan, Pierre Antoine. 2007. "Higher Education in Francophone Africa: What Tools Can Be Used to Support Financially Sustainable Policies?" Working Paper 135. World Bank, Washington, DC.

InterAcademy Council. 2004. "Inventing a Better Future." Amsterdam: InterAcademy Council. http://www.interacademycouncil.net/?id=10011.

Ledoux, Blandine, and Alain Mingat. 2007. "La soutenabilité financière comme référence pour le développement de l'éducation post-primaire dans les pays d'Afrique subsaharienne." Unpublished draft.

MINESUP (Ministère de l'Enseignement Supérieur du Cameroun). 2007. *Annuaire statistique 2006 de l'enseignement supérieur*. Yaoundé: MINESUP.

Mingat, Alain, and Bruno Suchaut. 2000. *African Educational Systems: A Comparative Economic Analysis*. Brussels: De Broeck University.

Mingat, Alain, Blandine Ledoux, and Ramahatra Rakotomalala. 2009. *Developing Post-primary Education in Sub-Saharan Africa: Assessing the Financial Sustainability of Alternative Pathways*. Paris: Agence Française de Développement; Washington, DC: World Bank.

Pôle de Dakar. 2008. "Réformes de l'enseignement supérieur en Afrique: Eléments de cadrages." Pôle de Dakar, BREDA, UNESCO, Dakar. http://www.poledakar.org.

Salmi, Jamil. 2008. *Financing and Governance of Tertiary Education in Madagascar*. Washington, DC: World Bank.

Uganda, Ministry of Education and Sports. 2006. *Uganda Education Statistics Abstract*. Vol. 1. Kampala: Republic of Uganda.

UNESCO (United Nations Educational, Scientific, and Cultural Organization), BREDA (Bureau for Education in Africa). 2005. *Education pour tous en Afrique: Repères pour l'action*. Dakar: UNESCO, BREDA.

———. 2007. *Education pour tous en Afrique: L'urgence de politiques sectorielles intégrées*. Dakar: UNESCO, BREDA.

Université de Bangui. 2008. "Quelques statistiques sur l'enseignement supérieur centrafricain." Document presented at the UNESCO Institute for Statistics Workshop on Statistics in Higher Education, Dakar. April.

World Bank. 2008a. *Accelerating Catch-up: Tertiary Education for Growth in Sub-Saharan Africa*. Washington, DC: World Bank.

———. 2008b. "RESEN [Rapport d'Etat du Système Educatif National]: Country Status Report; Benin." World Bank, Washington, DC.

———. 2009. *World Development Indicators*. Washington, DC: World Bank.

CHAPTER 3

Main Features of Current Funding Policies and Practices

Budget allocation practices, which cover both operating and investment budgets, remain largely traditional. Operating budgets cover expenditures that occur each year. Investment budgets cover expenditures that increase capital assets, such as buildings or equipment. The two types of budgets are usually managed separately.

Operating Budget Allocation Practices

The methods used by African governments to determine budgetary allocations for recurrent expenditures in higher education do not vary much across the continent. In most cases, initial allocation decisions are made by the Ministry of Finance in light of available government revenues, political priorities, and the amounts provided in the previous year. Having determined the general allocation, subsequent budget meetings with the Ministry of (Higher) Education and the universities tend to be formalities. In spite of the magnitude of financial need confronting the institutions, the margin for considering a significant adjustment to the Ministry of Finance's allocated amount is minimal. Consequently, budget discussions often focus on minor adjustments to the internal distribution of these fixed allocations among staff salaries, student services, staff development, and operational expenses. Overall, the methods of determining budget allocations for higher education resemble those carried over from the colonial period. Too often, the entire process of budget development—a sequence of submission, review, and approval steps that rise through the university hierarchy and up ministry and government hierarchies—is little more than an annual ritual.

The consequence of maintaining outdated practices presents the higher education sector with formidable challenges (see box 3.1). The procedures are rigid and frustrate efforts to adopt good practices from other higher education systems or to adjust to shifting circumstances. Where imbalances and inequities characterize funding patterns among institutions, these practices do not allow for any redress. In addition, the traditional approaches do

---

Box 3.1

Budget Allocation Practices in Mali

In Mali, budget allocations for higher education depend on practices that are largely beyond the control of individual institutions or even the Ministry of Education. The allocation amounts are derived by multiplying the number of academic staff positions authorized for an institution by an associated expense factor. Academic staff members are public employees, and their salaries—23 percent of higher education expenditures—are determined by public service pay scales. The Ministry of Finance pays staff salaries directly, and these amounts do not come under the control of universities. Similarly, student services allocations—48 percent of higher education expenditures—are based on the number of students multiplied by a per capita expense factor that is the result of a series of contested agreements between student associations and government representatives. The portion of the budget earmarked for scholarships to enable university study abroad—8 percent of higher education expenditures—is allocated and managed separately from other higher education expenditures and is not linked to institutional needs for staff development or to shortages of labor market skills. As a result, university leaders have limited resources—representing just 21 percent of the operating budget—to manage in accordance with the priority needs or strategic objectives of their institution. Moreover, fragmentation of budget management among several institutions leaves the government with few means of encouraging better institutional performance, more efficient use of funds, or a strategic approach to budgeting.

Sources: Brossard and Foko 2008.

not provide any incentives for improved institutional performance or greater efficiency in the use of scarce resources. Moreover, they are not linked in any way to national development objectives or human resource needs. These shortcomings constitute major handicaps at a time when competition among higher education institutions is increasing both within and among countries and when governments are seeking greater institutional accountability in the use of public funds.

A range of practices for determining higher education budget allocations for recurrent and investment expenditures can be found around the world. In addition to historically based budgeting, they include earmarked funding, input-based formulas, performance-based formulas, performance contracts, and competitive funds. Although some African countries have experimented with these other approaches, they are exceptions. Most African nations have yet to attempt any innovation in their budget allocation methods. Table 3.1 provides a preliminary classification of countries with regard to the type of allocation methods they use for higher education.

Historically Based Budgeting

The most common approach to operational budgeting for universities is to use the previous year or years as a baseline and make incremental changes based on general considerations such as the country's economic performance, government revenues, inflation rates, or institutional growth.[1] This approach was widespread in Africa during the 1990s (Ade Ajayi, Goma, and Ampah Johnson 1996; Mwiria 2003) and continues today in Ethiopia, Lesotho, Madagascar, Mauritania, Mozambique, Sudan, Zimbabwe, and most other countries (Lewin, Ntoi, and Puleng Mapuru 2000; Orr 2002; Kharchi 2003; Merisotis 2003; Salmi 2008).[2]

This historically referenced procedure can evolve into "negotiated budgeting" when institutional leaders seek to influence government decisions with regard to incremental changes in their budgets. The final amounts are unlikely to vary much from historical levels, but they may be somewhat enhanced as the result of special circumstances, political considerations, or the negotiators' skills of persuasion (Jongbloed 2000). Because of revenue constraints, such negotiations are unlikely to influence allocation decisions by the Ministry of Finance. However, once the general budgetary allocation for the education sector has been made, university leaders may occasionally argue successfully for marginal increments in their share. But where staff salaries depend on public service pay scales or agreements with academic staff unions and where levels of student

Table 3.1 Methods of Allocating the Higher Education Budget in Select African Countries

Operating budget			Investment budget		
Historically based budgets	Input-based budgets	Funding formula	Performance contracts	Earmarked funding	Competitive funds
Angola	Ghana	South Africa	Côte d'Ivoire[b]	South Africa	Ethiopia
Benin	Kenya		Mali[b]		Ghana
Burkina Faso	Mauritius[a]		Mauritania[b]		Mozambique
Burundi	Mozambique		Senegal[b]		South Africa
Cameroon	Nigeria				Tanzania[a]
Central African Republic	Rwanda				
Chad	Tanzania				
Congo, Dem. Rep. of	Uganda				
Eritrea					
Ethiopia					
Gabon					
Gambia, The					
Lesotho					
Liberia					
Madagascar					
Malawi					
Mali					
Mauritania					
Namibia					
Niger					
Sierra Leone					
Sudan					
Swaziland					
Togo					
Zambia					
Zimbabwe					

Source: Authors.
a. In process of implementation (Pillay 2008 for Mauritius; World Bank 2008b for Tanzania).
b. Announced, but current implementation status is uncertain.

services are worked out in response to confrontations with student associations, the budgetary space for negotiation is severely limited.

Input-based Formulas

As governments move away from historical budgets, they are likely to adopt some type of input measure as the basis for budgeting (see box 3.2). The most basic input used is the number of staff or staff salaries, with the

> **Box 3.2**
>
> **Line Item Budgeting in Uganda**
>
> In Uganda, public funds for each higher education institution are provided in three blocks: one for baseline salaries, one for development costs, and one for operating expenditure (based on a set amount per student per day and intended to cover mainly food and housing for students). The baseline salary block is calculated by reference to the number of posts agreed by the government. Apart from the two public universities, the number of posts, by grade and by discipline, is set by the Ministry of Public Service, which also sets the salary levels. The two public universities have more flexibility, but most of their public funds are still calculated by reference to the number of posts at predetermined government grades. For each institution, each block of funds is then broken down into line items, producing a total of about 30 budget line items. Each of these is then reviewed line by line with the Ministry of Finance. Institutions are then expected to spend their public funds within the approved line item breakdown, although the movement of funds between lines is possible with prior Ministry of Finance approval.
>
> *Source:* Thompson 2001.

nonsalary portion of the budget determined as a set percentage of the total payroll. Alternatively, student enrollment may be used by multiplying the number of students by the average cost per student. These represent the simplest kind of formula funding.

Costs per student can be calculated in several ways (Salmi and Hauptman 2006). One is the actual costs per student in prior years as reported by the institution. Kenya and Rwanda employ variations of this method.[3] In Kenya, however, the result of the student cost-based formula calculation is apparently open to subsequent negotiation between university leaders and the Ministry of Finance (Otieno 2008). As a result, the amounts per student received by each university vary substantially, even though the use of a common unit-cost formula would suggest that the allocations per student should be the same. Specifically, in 2005, funding per student for six Kenyan public universities ranged from US$1,962 to US$2,989 (Otieno 2008). Lack of a clear relationship between student enrollment and budgetary allocations has also been observed in Tanzania and other countries (World Bank 2008a, 2008b).

A second alternative is to use the average cost per student for the higher education system as a whole. This requires a capacity to generate aggregate statistics on enrollment and recurrent expenditures—classified consistently—in all institutions, but this entails an efficiency incentive for outlying performers, as institutions with average costs above the norm will not have their full costs funded.

The third approach is to calculate normative unit costs (see box 3.3). In this, optimal student-staff ratios and other efficiency standards are used to calculate what costs per student ought to be rather than what they actually are. Normative cost formulas hold a strong potential for improving systemwide efficiency because they link how much each institution will receive to a uniform efficiency-based standard. But they also promote uniformity instead of diversity and innovation among institutions as a result of norm-based micro management by government. This approach has been employed in Nigeria and Ghana. Normative cost formulas are derived from two main variables: the prescribed student-teacher ratio by discipline and the recommended costs of goods and services for a teaching unit by discipline.[4] In Ghana, the normative cost calculations have tended

---

Box 3.3

Normative Input-based Budgeting in Nigeria

The National Universities Commission in Nigeria has long employed a normative approach to input-based budgeting for Nigeria's federal universities. In calculating an institution's budget recommendation, academic staff numbers are derived from student numbers using normative guidelines for student-staff ratios that vary by discipline. Likewise, administrative support staff numbers are determined from academic staff numbers using similar guidelines. Thereafter, total compensation (salaries and allowances) is computed and becomes the basis for calculating the figure for goods and services. The value of goods and services for each faculty is equal to 20 percent of salaries for arts faculties and 30 percent for science faculties. Additionally, this item is inflated for postgraduate students by applying an extra weighting of 0.4. Finally, universities are encouraged to set aside 1 percent of their recurrent grant as a contingency for supporting the pension scheme. Additionally, 10 percent of each university's recurrent grant is to be devoted to the development of that institution's library, and 5 percent is earmarked for research. The National Universities Commission releases these latter two portions of the total recurrent grant (library and research funds) separately, subject to satisfactory accounting for the appropriate use of the previous quarter's release.

Source: Hartnett 2000.

to run about 60 percent higher than the actual level of funding provided to institutions by the Ministry of Finance. This sizable imbalance generates efficiency pressures through significant underfunding rather than through the application of realistic norms (Adu and Orivel 2006). The result is across-the-board belt tightening rather than strategic adjustment.

Irrespective of the type of cost-per-student method that is employed, the delineation of costs by field and level of study is a useful consideration. On the basis of careful systemwide analyses of expenditure patterns by disciplinary area and type of degree program, agreement is reached on appropriate costs per student for each. Tanzania has used this method. For example, postgraduate costs per student are frequently higher than undergraduate costs per student, taking into account the smaller class size, increased need for student advising, and more intensive use of libraries and laboratories associated with postgraduate studies. Likewise, courses that are largely based on lectures (for example, history, sociology, literature) usually have lower costs per student than those that require extensive laboratory work or field practice (for example, chemistry, engineering, veterinary medicine). When such distinctions are made in the budgeting process, governments frequently cluster disciplines with similar unit costs into a limited number of cost categories to simplify the budget formula. This is the approach employed in South Africa (Pillay 2008).

Performance-based Formulas

A much rarer approach to budget calculation incorporates output measures into the formula. Commonly used indicators are the number of graduates, the rate of student repetition, the number of minority, women, or regionally disadvantaged students who are admitted, and research productivity. Performance-based formulas differ from other budgeting methods in that their indicators often reflect public policy objectives rather than institutional needs. In addition, they may include incentives for institutional improvement instead of reinforcing the status quo, as is often characteristic of more traditional allocation mechanisms (Salmi and Hauptman 2006).

Since the 1990s, governments around the world have increasingly used performance-based funding models to steer universities (Sorlin 2007). This method avoids the use of autonomy-limiting policy directives, and instead of stipulating certain activities, it simply makes them financially attractive (Orr 2005). In Africa, however, experimentation with performance-based formulas has been muted and apparently limited to South Africa (see box 3.4). However, Botswana, Ethiopia, Mozambique,

Box 3.4

Formula Funding in South Africa

South Africa's 10-year-old funding formula combines performance-based formulas, earmarked funding, and block grants. The approach distributes to institutions the funds made available by government in ways that advance policy priorities. Funding is not intended to cover specific institutional needs or levels of cost, as in some other formulas. Rather, it pays institutions for delivering teaching and research services specified in government-approved plans.

Block grants comprise (a) teaching funds calculated by student enrollment and costs per student for different subject matter categories, (b) teaching funds based on agreed teaching outputs (for example, improved graduation rates), (c) research funds for agreed outputs, and (d) institutional factor funds for enrolling students from disadvantaged groups, maximizing enrollment capacity, and attaining enrollment consistent with government-designated priority areas. Institutions are informed in advance of the total amount of the block grant they will receive.

Earmarked funds are designated for specific purposes. In the main, these are for the national student financial aid scheme, research development, foundational programs, teaching development, approved capital projects, and interest payments on approved loans.

The advantages of this approach are its predictability, incentives for efficiency, capacity to operate within hard budget constraints, and promotion of institutional autonomy and equity. In South Africa, its principal difficulties relate to obtaining "buy-in" from institutions, as some feared that the budget would be reduced under the new formula, while others feared that the approach would not achieve its intended results. A consultative process managed by the Ministry of Education and the South African Universities Vice-Chancellors Association eased these anxieties and softened initial institutional resistance to the change.

Four lessons can be drawn from the South African experience: (a) simplicity is the key to success, and the formula should be understood by the broadest possible segment of the higher education community; (b) consultation is required to foster understanding and acceptance of the formula and should be followed by appropriate training of key university staff; (c) effective data management systems within institutions and government are necessary to ensure that the formula is implemented correctly and transparently; and (d) linkages between higher education and the labor market are needed to monitor the relevance of higher education outputs and outcomes.

Sources: Pillay 2004, 2008.

and Tanzania are reportedly considering a move to funding-formula budgeting, but decisions are still pending, and in some cases have been for several years.

The choice of which budgeting modality to employ has significant ramifications, as summarized in table 3.2. Each encourages a different type of behavior, each requires different capacities to generate institutional statistics and to interpret the results, and each ultimately has a different impact on sector performance. At one extreme, historically based budgeting is comparatively easy to implement from a technical viewpoint, but is apt to maintain the existing system regardless of its shortcomings. At the other extreme, performance-based budgeting requires a greater capacity to generate data and develop performance indicators, but encourages those systems able to do so with the tools needed to foster quality and relevance.

Investment Budget Allocation Practices

Allocation decisions with regard to the investment budgets of higher education institutions generally appear to be made through somewhat more transparent and rational procedures. Often, construction on university campuses has been planned, prioritized, and costed within the institution's approved physical development plan. In turn, system oversight bodies develop their own list of investment priorities for the overall subsector. However, it also seems that investment allocation decision making may be more open to negotiation and outside influence on

Table 3.2 Budgeting Modalities

Budgeting modality	Key feature	Requirements for data and technical expertise	Impact on sector performance
Historically based	Rewards negotiation skills	Minimal	Maintains status quo
Input based	Rewards expansion of inputs	Moderate	Encourages growth
Normative	Rewards adherence to defined norms	Moderate	Encourages uniformity
Performance based	Rewards outcome achievements	Considerable	Encourages quality and relevance

Source: Authors.

behalf of university authorities, as investment projects are not so susceptible to pressure from interest groups operating budgets are. For instance, the quiet administrative replacement of a road resurfacing project with a university classroom construction project is unlikely to provoke much clamor. Three relatively recent mechanisms for allocating investment funds—earmarked funding, performance contracts, and competitive funds—respond to this problem by incorporating more explicit and transparent decision-making criteria.

Earmarked Funding

Earmarking—also called set-asides, reserved funding, or special-purpose funding—is another means of allocating public funds to higher education institutions. In this case, the government designates or "earmarks" a particular institution or group of institutions to receive funds for a specific purpose. Frequently, earmarked or reserved funds are used as a way of correcting perceived inequities in past funding patterns (Salmi and Hauptman 2006). For example, in the immediate post-apartheid period, South Africa set aside funds for libraries, academic facilities, and equipment for predominantly black institutions before subsequent institutional mergers were enacted. In some cases, earmarked funds are paid out on the basis of specified measures of performance. This is the current practice in South Africa, where funds are reserved for teaching and research, but allocations are based in part on institutional performance in these areas. However, the limited African experience with earmarked funding apparently has been restricted to universities and not yet applied to other institutions for professional and technical education.

Performance Contracts

Under this method, governments enter into mutual agreements with institutions to fund them in return for achieving certain performance goals. All or part of the funding may be based on whether institutions meet the targets stipulated in the contracts. Within Africa, several countries (for example, Côte d'Ivoire, Mauritania, and Senegal) have experimented with this mechanism, but it has yet to be adopted as a better way of allocating funds.

South Africa has developed its own version of a "funding contract" approach. Its funding framework is a distributive mechanism—that is, it serves as a way of allocating government funds to individual institutions in accordance with both the budget made available by government and with the government's policy priorities (that is, teaching and research outputs specified in government-approved plans). The framework is not dependent on either calculations of actual institutional costs or on normative calculations for efficient universities. It recognizes that institutional costs tend to be a function of income: whatever is available will be spent. Government funding for institutions of higher education is therefore not designed to meet specific types or levels of institutional cost, but rather to pay institutions for delivering the teaching- and research-related services specified by government-approved plans. Institutions then have the freedom to design their activities in line with the funds provided to them (Pillay 2004). Among the advantages of the South African budgeting mechanism are predictability, recognition of university autonomy, incentives for efficiency, adjustments for equity considerations, and recognition of the very real constraints on the availability of public revenues for higher education (Pillay 2008).

Competitive Funds

Various governments have chosen to supplement the core budgets of universities by using nonbudgetary mechanisms to provide incentives in the form of additional investment resources. Because this funding comes on top of the regular budget, it constitutes attractive discretionary money that can be used flexibly to pursue innovation or address special needs. One common form of budget supplementation is the competitive fund. Initially used to fund research, this instrument has now been adapted to stimulate quality improvements, new initiatives, partnerships, and other ways of adapting to change within universities and polytechnics. It normally functions on the basis of institutional or departmental funding proposals that are subjected to anonymous peer review using publicly announced evaluation criteria to assess their merits. Competitive funds are used for investment purposes in Ethiopia, Ghana, Mozambique, and South Africa.

Budget Management Practices and the Optimal Use of Available Resources

Capable budget management across the tertiary subsector is necessary for budgeting processes to achieve their intended results. However, inefficient application of funds by both governments and higher education institutions often dilutes the impact of funds provided. This is the consequence of numerous factors, including the absence of defined funding mechanisms (such as formulas), poor planning, poor oversight (including of student loan schemes), poor monitoring of expenditures, excessive public expenditure on students studying overseas, inefficient use of available funds (as demonstrated by high student dropout and repetition rates), high proportions of overhead and salary expenses for nonacademic staff, and high levels of institutional debt (for example, Nigeria, Zambia). In addition to the problem of inefficient resource use, other budget management issues include lack of transparency in decision making, fragmented budget responsibilities, and inability to rein in out-of-control higher education budgets.

Central Management

In numerous cases, higher education budgets are administered directly by the Ministry of Education (more commonly in small countries) or by the Ministry of Finance (for example, direct payment of salary and benefits). In such cases, universities have little opportunity to implement their own development strategies, manage staff on the basis of performance, or adapt to changing circumstances. Countries in which all or part of the university budget is centrally managed include Benin, Burkina Faso, Ethiopia, and Gabon. Cameroon, Côte d'Ivoire, Mali, and the Democratic Republic of Congo modify this approach by having the Ministry of Finance appoint the university's accounting officer as a ministry employee to maintain the control function.

Where central management of the budget is prominent, institutional managers may have limited control over their own institutional budgets because portions of it are administered by other public entities (for example, salaries, student welfare, electricity). While perhaps more common in Francophone countries, this can be a problem in Anglophone countries as well. For example, grants for 5,250 students in Lesotho are administered by the Ministry of Finance, although they are considered part of education sector expenditure (Pillay 2008).

Diffuse Management

In other cases, the budget for higher education is spread across two or more ministries. This makes coordinated sector strategies and coherent policy development exceedingly difficult. This occurs most often when traditional universities fall under the purview of the ministry of education, specialized universities are housed within the ministries of agriculture or health, and dedicated postsecondary training institutes are incorporated within other ministries. For example, in Nigeria, funding for postsecondary education is spread across 17 ministries (World Bank 2006a).

Tanzania has recently tackled the problem of dispersed management of higher education. Until February 2008, government functions with respect to higher education were assigned to the Ministry of Higher Education, Science, and Technology (MHEST), while the Ministry of Education and Vocational Training (MoEVT) held responsibility for postsecondary technical and teacher education. At that time, MHEST was dissolved, and its higher education functions were transferred to MoEVT. This decision concentrated responsibility for the largest tertiary institutions within a single ministry. However, 19 other public tertiary technical institutes remain attached to various other ministries. To manage this problem, the government created an interministerial Tertiary and Higher Education Development Committee to bring greater coordination to tertiary education. Although these steps reduce the diffusion of management responsibilities for the subsector, the consolidation is clearly not yet complete.

Within the Francophone region, the establishment of separate ministries of higher education has often provided a mechanism for bringing together under a single supervisory authority several higher education institutions previously scattered under several government ministries.[5] However, this solution has not completely resolved the problem of diffuse management, as in virtually all cases the sizable portion of the budget allocated to student services (commonly 25–50 percent) is managed independently by a Centre National des Oeuvres Universitaires (National Agency for University Affairs) over which institutions and even ministries have little influence. This is because the center is legally constituted in various countries (for example, Benin, Côte d'Ivoire, and Mali) as a financially autonomous organization that reports directly to the minister.

Delegated Management

As higher education systems have expanded in terms of enrollment and number of institutions, governments have felt the need to delegate to separate statutory entities the responsibilities of managing routine activities and monitoring the performance of tertiary institutions. Sometimes these entities take the form of semiautonomous "buffer bodies" accountable to the minister of education and called "national commissions for higher education" or "tertiary education councils." In other cases, governments create a separate ministry of higher education to carry out these functions. Whereas the buffer bodies often allow for greater coordination of overall education sector strategy and the use of specialized professional staff, ministries of higher education tend to compete with ministries of education, use generalist employees from the public service, and be somewhat more politically oriented in their handling of higher education matters. Within Africa, buffer bodies are more likely to be found in Anglophone countries, whereas ministries of higher education are more likely to be found in Francophone countries (see table 3.3). However, Rwanda has recently adopted the buffer body model. A total of 30 African countries have set up one of these two types of dedicated entities to oversee higher education.

Strategic Planning

Under the delegated management approach, institutional and even subsectorwide strategic plans are being used increasingly to guide budget allocation and management decision making. In a few countries, universities are required to submit a strategic plan along with their budget to the sector oversight body (Lesotho and Mauritius). In others, a national strategy for higher education shapes the budget determination process (Mozambique and South Africa). In both cases, reference to a strategic framework helps to align institutional funding with national development priorities.

Scenario Construction

Whether it is the result of a national strategy formulation process or an initiative by the national planning agency, the construction of medium- or long-term scenarios can provide a useful framework for decision making in higher education. These scenarios strive to project the size, shape, and cost of a future higher education system that is both responsive to the country's evolving needs for high-level skills and financially sustainable. This management tool has rarely been employed for higher education in Sub-Saharan Africa, although South Africa's Council on Higher Education and various donor agencies have used it to some extent. Recently, World Bank–financed studies have generated future financial scenarios based on enrollment trends and other assumptions for higher education in Benin, Burundi, Ghana, Mali, and Mauritania. These have had mixed results with regard to

Table 3.3 Entity in Charge of Higher Education Oversight, by Language Area

Type of entity	Anglophone	Francophone	Total
Higher education oversight entity	13	1	14
Ministry of higher education	3	13	16

Sources: International Association of Universities 2007; internal World Bank documentation.

their capacity to catalyze political attention to the need for policy reforms. Experience demonstrates that where the highest level of political decision making (prime minister or head of state) can be shown the political costs of maintaining present policies, significant shifts in policy are likely to result. For example, higher education scenario building in Mali carried out under the direct supervision of the prime minister triggered some reform proposals. In Burundi, the sector minister was an active participant in the process and arranged for the results to be presented to the Council of Ministers and to the National Assembly, subsequently launching a major reform effort. But where the scenario exercise fails to engage the highest political authorities, its potential benefits have been left unrealized. This point is illustrated by experience from Benin in early 2009, where scenario building was handled by a ministerial team created for this purpose. Although the work was reportedly well done and the resulting scenarios made realistic political, economic, and social projections, the final report was received by the sector minister and subsequently not acted upon. On the one hand, it appears that too much of the understanding gained from this exercise remained within the work team, which had little capacity to influence higher-level policy decisions. On the other hand, even sector ministers may not possess sufficient authority to make decisions that are likely to have substantial social (and therefore political) repercussions.

Mechanisms for the Transfer of Allocated Resources
No matter how budget allocation is carried out, expenditure is often implemented in ways that curtail efficiency and responsiveness. In many cases, budget resources are made available to recipient institutions through line item distribution, in which relatively rigid rules restrict spending to that particular item and regulate the extent to which funds may be switched from one line item to another. Once the budget is approved, authority to modify it may be centrally controlled by the ministry of finance or the ministry of education, or it may be delegated to the institution. In some instances, a single *block grant*, often distributed in quarterly shares, is used to transfer budgetary resources to the institution. This disbursement procedure, based on a single line item budget, is used in Kenya, South Africa, and Swaziland (Pillay 2004, 2008; Taskforce for the Development of the National Strategy for University Education 2008). Block grants give institutions more flexibility and autonomy in financial management than line item arrangements (Salmi and Hauptman 2006). Notably, some African governments (Ghana) claim to employ block grant allocations, although in practice disbursements may be monthly and government auditors may

challenge budget management practices that deviate from civil service norms (Girdwood 1999).

Institutional Budget Management

Flexibility in the management of an institution's own budget is an essential complement to institutional autonomy and governance reforms. If institutions are not permitted to undertake internal budget reallocations in response to emerging opportunities or shifting circumstances, they will lack a fundamental tool for implementing strategic decisions. In such cases, greater autonomy in institutional governance and management is a reform without means of expression.

Budget management flexibility for institutions in principle includes the following: (a) the ability to set and differentiate salaries on the basis of merit and performance, (b) the ability to shift salaries (and therefore staffing positions) among different faculties and departments, (c) the ability to reallocate funds from salaries to operating needs, and (d) the ability to retain savings and carry unspent balances over from one year to the next. In the absence of such flexibility, an institution loses the ability to be either strategic or efficient.

Despite a general lack of funding for research and quality investment, some countries have invested in ambitious policies. Current expenditure on research and development (R&D) in most African countries is too small to support focused and effective research outputs to address national development needs.[6] However, country-specific examples have shown that there are signs of a turnaround in the interest placed on research and higher education, as consensus is growing on the importance of building knowledge networks, global information resources, and technology transfer capacity.

In recent years, some countries have taken a reinvigorating approach to R&D. Rwanda, a frontrunner in information technology (IT), has boosted its expenditure on science to 1.6 percent of gross domestic product (GDP) and is aiming for 3 percent within the next five years (Steen 2008). Rwanda hosted the Connect Africa Summit in Kigali in October 2007 and brought together 500 of the world's leading actors in information technology. Nigeria is developing a Plan of Action for Science, Technology, and Innovation that government will use as a framework to guide investment at the national level and dialogue with donors. Among the major recommendations approved by the government is the creation of a US$5 billion endowment fund for the establishment of the National Science Foundation of Nigeria (see box 3.5). Mozambique, in a science and technology (S&T) strategy report of 2006, committed to achieving an

Box 3.5

Research Funding in Nigeria

What is known of research in Nigeria suggests that the limited funding allocated is spread thinly among a large number of organizations and institutions, with little strategic focus. Much of the research carried out in Nigeria occurs in the university setting, with 59 universities performing research (26 federal, 23 state, and 10 private) and 44 polytechnics recognized as centers for R&D activities. The federal institutions together with the research institutes receive about 1 percent of the federal budget, an allocation that is considerably below what is needed to support its operations, particularly in capital-intensive R&D operations in areas such as biotechnology, space research, and information technology. For 2004, the approved recurrent budget of the ministry was ₦3,352,167,903 (US$26 million at ₦1 = US$0.00780001), constituting 0.6 percent of the national recurrent budget of ₦539,286,472,751 (US$4.206 billion). This is significantly lower than the 1980 Lagos Plan of Action's target of 1 percent of GDP by 2000. The recent move to provide federal universities with targeted funding for research equipment from the Education and Training Foundation is a welcome intervention.

Source: World Bank 2006a.

S&T expenditure level of 0.8 percent of GDP by 2010 (Mozambique Council of Ministers 2006). Since 2003, the Ghana Education Trust (GET) Fund, financed through 2.5 percent of the prevailing value added tax, has been making funds available to tertiary education institutions for research and staff development through the National Council for Tertiary Education, prioritizing S&T, medical, and engineering faculties. See box 3.6 for research funding for agriculture.

Private Funding for Tertiary Education

Against a backdrop of growing demand for higher education and insufficient public supply, some governments and institutions have introduced fees and reduced social support services, boosting the participation of households in education expenses. In addition, the private higher education sector has grown rapidly, and public higher education institutions have diversified their sources of funding. To accompany these major changes in financing, some governments have developed student support policies such as student loans and other assistance programs.

> **Box 3.6**
>
> **Research Funding for Agriculture**
>
> In recent years, various African countries have undertaken efforts to move away from government dependency and establish broader partnerships and competitiveness strategies for agricultural research. For example, in 2004 the Kenyan government launched its 2004–14 Strategy for Revitalizing Agriculture, in which the objective of the research component is "to reform the agricultural research subsector so that it encompasses a plurality of actors to enhance efficiency and accountability." Another example is the Ugandan National Agricultural Research Bill of September 2005, which introduces important changes to the funding, performance, and dissemination of agricultural research. The National Agricultural Research Council oversees the allocation of a core research budget, 30 percent of which is allocated competitively to any qualified research group. This new policy ends a monopoly on research funding previously held by government-owned agricultural research institutes. The increased competition is expected to improve policy and relevance. Six new "zonal" research institutes are being created across the country to assure the relevance of research to the particular needs of agroecological zones.
>
> *Source:* World Bank 2007a; International Centre for development oriented Research in Agriculture, http://www.icra-edu.org.

Household Contribution

Households contribute approximately one-fourth of national expenditure (household and state outlays) on higher education (see figure 3.1). Unfortunately, this estimate is based on a sample of 18 countries for which information is available and this contribution would probably be higher if more states were taken into account, particularly English-speaking countries, where private instruction is more developed and school fees are generally higher. The share contributed by households varies widely, from less than 10 percent in Mali, Chad, and the Republic of Congo to about 60 percent in Uganda and Guinea-Bissau. More precise information regarding the contribution of households is crucial to formulating effective and fair policies for student support through scholarships or loans.

However, household financing for higher education is relatively limited compared to household investment in education at other levels of instruction, with primary and lower secondary education absorbing about 30 percent and 45 percent of national expenditure, respectively (see figure 3.2). This is a specifically African trait and contributes to

Figure 3.1 Share of Households in National Expenditure on Higher Education in Select African Countries, 2004 (or Closest Year)

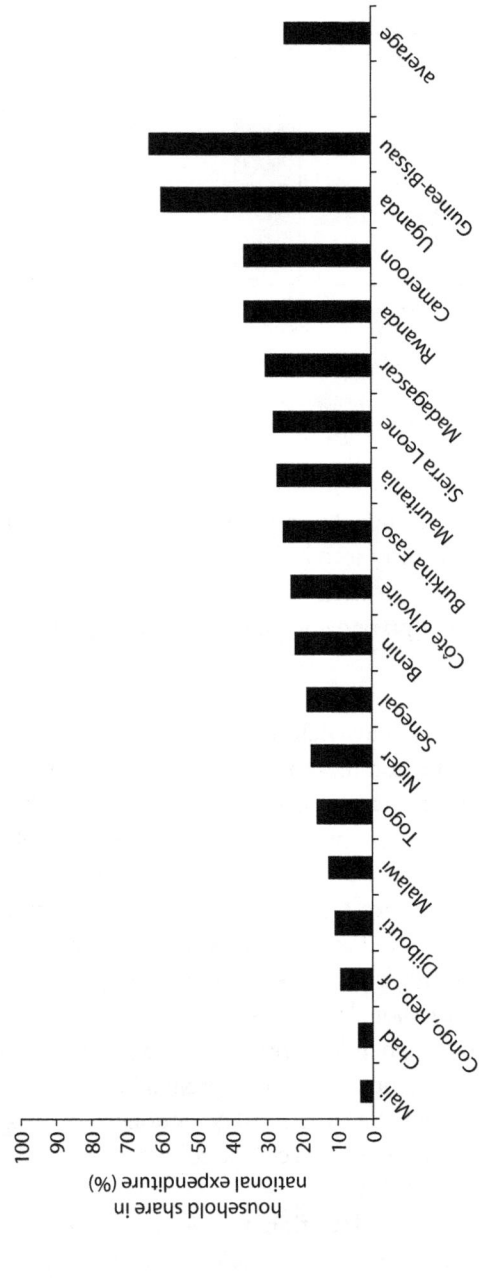

Source: Pôle de Dakar unpublished data; World Bank 2009a, 2009b.

Figure 3.2 Average Share of Households in National Expenditure on Education in 18 African Countries, by Level of Instruction, 2004 (or Closest Year)

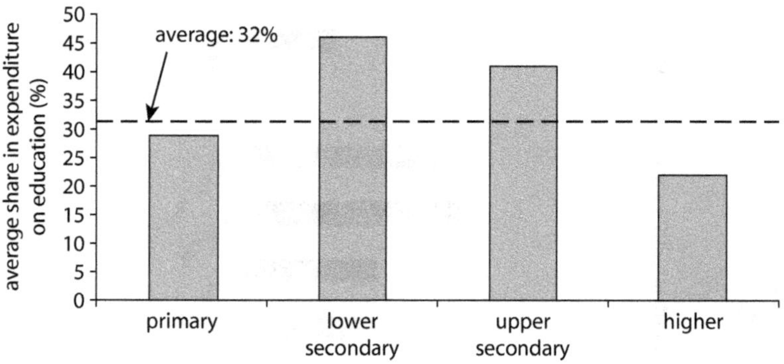

[Bar chart showing average share in expenditure on education (%) by level: primary ~29%, lower secondary ~46%, upper secondary ~41%, higher ~22%; dashed line at average: 32%]

Sources: World Bank 2009a, 2009b.
Note: On average, households in the countries considered contribute one-third (32 percent) of the national expenditure on education (all instruction levels combined), namely, an amount approximately equal to half of public expenditure on education.

inequality in the educational system by encouraging selection based on family resources before entry into higher education. A policy aimed at ensuring broader access to education should provide free basic education and increase the share of private contributions at the level of higher education.

Fee Policies

Cost-sharing policies may include, among others, the introduction of or major increases in tuition fees to cover part of the cost of instruction or the introduction of user charges to cover more of the cost of housing, food, and other student living expenses previously borne largely by governments (taxpayers) or institutions (Johnstone 2003).[7] Other less dramatic and politically explosive forms of cost sharing include the introduction of small, noninstructional charges such as registration, examination, or student activity fees, the freezing of or reduction in student support grants, the orientation (occasionally with some government funding) of students toward the tuition-dependent private sector, and in the few countries implementing significant student loan programs, an improvement in recovery rates (thereby reducing the need for public subsidies) through higher interest charges or more effective debt collection (Johnstone 2004).

Tuition fees. The type of tuition fee policy adopted by a country has implications for the assistance policies that are put in place to ensure access for its most vulnerable groups. Typically, an "up-front tuition policy" (and/or registration fees) requires students (or parents or extended families) to pay a tuition fee for a semester or academic year at the beginning of that semester or year. Sometimes the proportion of tuition fee to be paid or the amount of financial assistance available depends on a family's income. As shown in table 3.4, the number of African countries where up-front tuition fees have been introduced is growing, even in some Francophone countries such as Côte d'Ivoire and the Democratic Republic of Congo, where free higher education has long been considered an untouchable right.

As of 2009, in contrast to just a few years ago, at least 26 countries in Africa charge some type of tuition fee.[8] Table 3.4 presents information on the type of tuition fee policies being implemented in select African countries and the amount and financial significance of tuition fees charged. Burundi, Cameroon, Cape Verde, the Central African Republic, Chad, the Republic of Congo, Eritrea, Guinea, Mali, Mauritania, Niger, Nigeria (at the federal level), Sudan, and Togo do not charge tuition fees or charge insignificant ones.

Governments throughout the world that face either legal restrictions against or strong popular resistance to tuition fees often turn to "dual-track tuition policies," whereby a certain number of free (or almost free) university places are awarded by the government based on some criteria and other places are available on a tuition fee–paying basis. In Africa, two distinct types of dual-track tuition fee policies are being implemented. The first type, used in countries such as Ghana, Uganda (see box 3.7), Tanzania, and Kenya, awards free or low-cost places to a limited number of students based on their performance on the secondary school–leaving exam and fee-paying places to others who score lower but still meet entrance criteria or, as in Angola and Ethiopia, to those who study in the evening or during the summer. The second type, used in countries such as Benin (see box 3.8), Madagascar, and Senegal, offers free places to all students passing the high school–leaving baccalaureate exam in faculties with open access and fee-paying places in the more competitive professional faculties or institutions.

Another type of tuition policy that has been implemented in Africa is a "deferred tuition policy" wherein the tuition fee is expected from the student rather than from the family, but is deferred as a loan. Such a policy has the political advantage of somewhat disguising the implementation of a tuition fee, although it essentially forgoes some or perhaps most of the revenue that might be forthcoming from a family contribution that is attached to an "up-front" tuition fee.

Table 3.4 Types and Amounts of Tuition Fees in Public Higher Education Institutions

Country	Type of tuition fee policy	Amount of tuition fees[a]	Significance of tuition fees
Angola	Dual track	No tuition fees for regular students; tuition fees in evening study programs	No information
Benin	Dual track	No tuition fees in most programs; high fees in selective programs (CFAF 300,000 to CFAF 650,000)	Unit cost per university student is estimated at CFAF 280,900 to CFAF 1,001,200, or 65 to 90% of cost is covered by tuition fees in selective programs.
Botswana	Deferred	P 19,300 per year (2009–10 official exchange rate: US$7,975)	
Burkina Faso	Dual track	Most students: CFAF 15,000 (US$75) in fees; students at elite public institutions: up to €1,800 (not including room and board)	Tuition fees at elite institutions provide up to 50% of institutional income.
Côte d'Ivoire	Up-front	No information	No information
Ethiopia	Deferred	Br 869 to Br 1,998 (US$386 to US$888)	Deferred tuition fees are estimated at 15% of total instructional costs (actual recovery is uncertain).
Gabon	None or nominal	Not applicable	Not applicable
Gambia, The	Up-front	No information	Tuition fees cover up to 70% of university expenditures.
Ghana	Dual track: free tuition for regular students (but other fees are substantial), and tuition paid by fee-paying students	Regular students: free (but substantial fees); fee-paying students: ₵1,500 to ₵2,500 (US$1,083–US$1,806 at 2009 exchange rate)	Of the 30% of higher education funding that is to be raised by universities, a substantial portion would in theory come from tuition fees.

60

Kenya	Dual track and deferred (means tested): lower tuition fees for module I students, but up-front payment by all students	Module I: K Sh 16,000 (US$542); module II: average of K Sh 100,000 (US$3,387)	Module I: tuition fees are 19% of annual unit cost; module II: tuition fees are 50 to 100% of annual unit costs[b]; several public universities generate more than 30% of their income from tuition fees.
Lesotho	Deferred	M 8,500 (US$2,435)	Practically no recovery of deferred fees occurs.
Liberia	Up-front	$1,330 (US$2,714)	No information
Madagascar	Dual track: no tuition fees in most university programs, but higher fees in some professional programs; tuition fees in the two technology institutes and the business institute	Professional program: US$200 a year; technology institutes: US$50–US$160 a year; business institute: US$350 a year	Only 7% of higher education income comes from student tuition fees.
Malawi	Dual track: residential and nonresidential (those who are qualified for admission, but not admitted as residential students because of insufficient housing space)	Residential program: MK 25,000 (US$633); nonresidential: MK 100,000–MK 115,000 (US$2,534–US$2,914) plus room and board	Residential: tuition fees represent 8% of unit costs per student; nonresidential: tuition fees represent 35 to 40% of unit costs per student.
Mauritius	Dual track	No tuition fees for students at most higher education institutions; students at University of Technology and Mauritius College of Air: tuition fees of MUR 44,600 a year (US$3,038) compared to a unit cost per program of MUR 47,300 a year (US$3,222)	Tuition fees contribute a significant portion (94%) of unit costs at University of Technology and Mauritius College of Air.

(continued)

Table 3.4 Types and Amounts of Tuition Fees in Public Higher Education Institutions *(continued)*

Country	Type of tuition fee policy	Amount of tuition fees[a]	Significance of tuition fees
Mozambique	Up-front	US$100 a year	Tuition fees provide approximately 3% of the financial resources collected by public higher education institutions.
Namibia	Up-front Deferred (means tested)	2009 N$7,000 a year (US$1,643)	Tuition fees (2002) provide 23% of revenue of University of Namibia and 14% of revenue of Polytechnic; the share of annual spending per student (2001) is 25% at University of Namibia and 30% at Polytechnic.
Nigeria (state level)	Up-front	₦14,300 (Enugu State, 2001)	In 1998, total per student unit cost in Enugu State University was ₦29,763, so tuition fees cover almost half.
Rwanda	Deferred and dual track	Government-sponsored students: RF 100,000; privately paying students: band 1 (RF 530,000) to band 6 (RF 1,325,000 for programs such as medicine), or US$2,846 to US$7,116 in 2009	Government-supported students pay 6–8% of instructional costs per student; privately paying students cover approximately 25% of instructional costs for S&T courses and 50% for other courses.
Senegal	Dual track	No tuition fees in most programs; fees in selective programs	No information
Sierra Leone	Up-front	No information	No information
South Africa	Up-front	R 20,370–R 31,000 (US$5,263–US$8,010)	Student fees supply approximately 28% of higher education institutions' income (2004).
Swaziland	Deferred	US$1,105–US$1,200	University of Swaziland generates 20% of its income from student tuition fees.

Tanzania	Up-front (means tested) and dual track	T Sh 1 million–T Sh 1.5 million (US$2,577–US$3,791) in 2008/09	For recurrent expenditure, 10% of income comes from student fees (not limited to tuition fees).
Uganda	Dual track (merit based)	U Sh 500,000–U Sh 800,000 (US$806–US$1,291)	Tuition fees account for 48% of unit costs at Makerere University and about 56% of university income (2005/06) in the three public universities.
Zambia	Dual track (merit based)	K 2,983,500–K 3,685,500 (US$1,235–US$1,525) per semester for fee-paying students; government-sponsored students: grants for up to 75% of total education costs (fees, books, living allowances)	Tuition fees from fee-paying students account for 70 to close to 90% of recurrent unit costs
Zimbabwe	Dual track	Some payment by everyone; higher payment by parallel program students	Of recurrent expenditure 5% comes from student tuition fees.

Sources: For Benin, World Bank 2008c; for Botswana, Pillay 2008, University of Botswana 2009; for Burkina Faso, *University World News* 2009; for The Gambia, Materu 2007, "Re-visioning Africa's Tertiary Education in the Transition to a Knowledge Economy," *The Statesman*, April 27, 2007; for Ghana, Manuh, Gariba, and Budu 2007; for Kenya, Mwiria and others 2007, Munene and Otieno 2008, HESA 2008; for Lesotho, Pillay 2008, National University of Lesotho 2008; for Madagascar, Pillay 2008, Chilundo 2008; for Namibia, Pillay 2008, Adongo 2008; for Nigeria, Aina 2002; for South Africa, HESA 2008; for Swaziland, Pillay 2008; for Tanzania, University of Dar es Salaam 2009, Sokoine University of Agriculture (2009); for Uganda, Musisi 2007; for Zambia, Pillay 2008, University of Zambia 2008; for Zimbabwe, Pillay 2008.

Note: In US$ converted from currency of most recent year for which data are available using estimates from World Bank (2005).

a. Except where indicated, World Bank International Comparison Program global purchasing power parity conversions were used.

b. Annual unit cost for tuition estimated to be K Sh 86,000 but significantly underestimated and more than K Sh 180,000 in most programs.

Box 3.7

A Financial Revolution: Makerere University in Uganda

Government financing was maintained for a limited number of students, and a private entry scheme was introduced to cover remaining demand. Between 1997 and 2006, the number of students multiplied by 2.4, increasing from 14,400 to 34,500. During the same period, university financing changed profoundly (see figure below), and the share of private financing in the university budget grew from 30 to 60 percent. Public financing per student was maintained for government-sponsored students only, whose number increased from 6,710 to 6,948. However, these students represented a declining portion of the total number of students, falling from 46 to 20 percent, while the average public resources per student decreased by 50 percent. Nevertheless, this situation has improved since 2001. In sum, public and private resources per student have decreased 10 percent since 1997.

Box Figure   Financing and Resources per Student in Uganda, 1997–2006

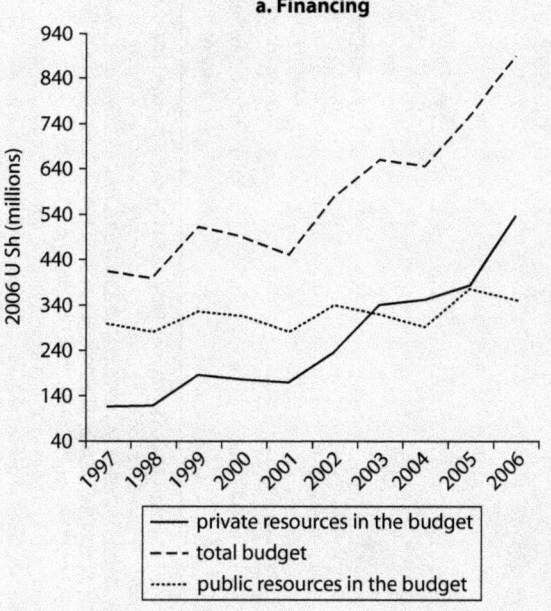

(continued)

Box 3.7 *(continued)*

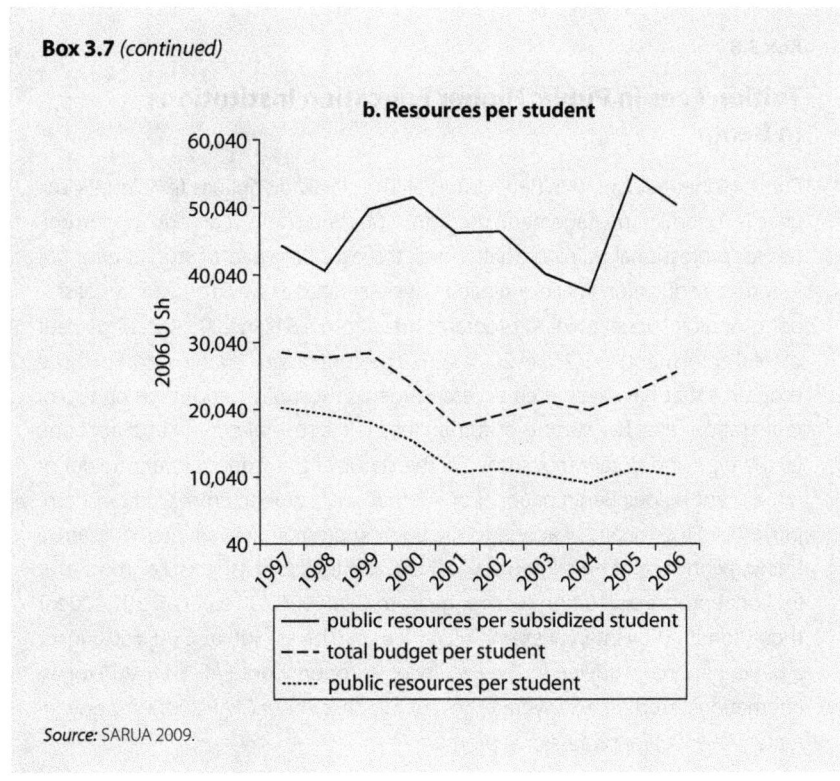

Source: SARUA 2009.

Because student loan schemes are generally used to cover student-borne costs of living (food, housing, and other essentials), there has been a juxtaposition between (a) tuition fees that are deferred (generally paid by the student) as opposed to up front (generally paid by families) and (b) income-contingent as opposed to fixed-schedule repayment obligations for students loans. This has led to considerable policy confusion. Income-contingent loans are generally thought to work best when they can be collected by employers at the point of wage or salary payments along with deductions for income tax withholding and insurance and pension obligations, as in Australia or the United Kingdom. The scheme works much less well in Sub-Saharan African countries, where tax identification numbers are not yet ubiquitous and where university graduates are much more likely to hold multiple jobs, be self-employed, or work outside the country. True deferred fees—wherein the students, regardless of parental wealth, are considered ultimately responsible for a share

> **Box 3.8**
>
> **Tuition Fees in Public Higher Education Institutions in Benin**
>
> Public higher education in Benin offers all the classic disciplines (law, letters, science, economics, management, medicine). Starting some years ago, opportunities for professional training (that is, two, three, or five years of studies after the secondary education final examination) were created as well. The number of students in professional training programs grew from 4,847 in 2002–03 (15 percent of total enrollment) to 9,215 in 2007–08 (20 percent of total enrollment). For those programs that have restricted access, students must pay tuition fees on top of registration fees. The setting of tuition fees takes several criteria into account: (a) the type and duration of study, (b) the status of the student (grant holder or not a grant holder, Benin national or international student, employed or unemployed), (c) the means of access to the training program (via an internal exam, a training contract, or enrollment by waiver), and (d) social aspects. For most professional programs, tuition fees range from CFAF 106,200 to CFAF 501,200 for those admitted by internal exam. Tuition fees can be as high as CFAF 650,000 for a Benin national studying in the Faculty of Agronomy or CFAF 1,444,200 for an international student. The average cost of tuition is about CFAF 300,000 (approximately US$600) for professional programs.

of higher education costs—exist in Africa, in only Botswana, Ethiopia, and Lesotho. In these three countries, all students who have been admitted to university may defer their tuition fees and repay them as a student loan following graduation or departure from the university.

The policies in Namibia (adopted in 1997), Rwanda (adopted in 2003, with means testing beginning in 2008), and Tanzania (adopted in 2005) conform more to a model of "up-front" tuition, in which parents are responsible for the higher education costs of their children, with a deferred fee option only available for needy students. Eligibility for the deferred fees with income-contingent repayment options are means tested based on parental income, and those students who are not eligible for the loan or who are eligible for only part of the loan have to pay their tuition fees up-front.

A graduate tax is a variant on the income-contingent loan, in which the student, in return for low or no tuition fees, becomes obligated after graduation to pay an income surtax, generally for the rest of his or her earning lifetime, with no "balances owed" and no way to prepay or exit the obligation (Johnstone 2006). While no country has a formal graduate tax at the present time,[9] the income-contingent repayment obligation in Ethiopia is actually called a "graduate tax."

Table 3.5 presents the financial significance of tuition fees for 17 countries where data are available. Tuition fees are categorized according to the proportion of instructional costs, recurrent costs, and institutional income.

Measuring the significance of tuition fees in terms of the cost burden they place on students and their families is problematic. In the absence of detailed income data, gross national income (GNI) per capita is sometimes used to represent average income. However, it does not capture the real situation because the extremely low GNI per capita estimates have little to do with the viability of the tuition fees. In Benin, for example, the tuition fees charged in the selective programs range from 104 to 225 percent of national income per capita, which would indicate that they are out of reach of most of the population. However, the average income of the typical

Table 3.5 Financial Significance of Tuition Fees in Select Countries

Insignificant (≤ 10%)	Significant (11–29%)	Very significant (>30%)
Tanzania+	Namibia◊	Benin (selective programs)+
Zimbabwe+	South Africa◊	Kenya (module II)+
Madagascar◊	Swaziland◊	Mauritius (University of Technology, Mauritius)+
Malawi (residential)+	Ethiopia*	
Mozambique◊	Kenya (module I)+	Uganda (fee paying)+
Rwanda (government supported)*	Rwanda (privately paying science courses)*	Zambia (fee paying)+
		Burkina Faso (elite institutions)◊
		Ghana◊
		Kenya◊
		Malawi (nonresidential)+
		Rwanda (privately paying nonscience courses)*
		Nigeria (state universities)+

Source: Authors.
Note: * = significance based on percentage of instructional cost; + = significance based on percentage of recurrent unit costs; ◊ = significance based on percentage of institutional income. The most accurate method of assessing the financial significance of tuition fees and the share of the institutional costs borne by students is to relate their tuition fees to the costs of instruction (from which nonteaching-related expenses such as research and services have been deducted). However, such data are rarely available in developing countries (Ziderman and Albrecht 1995) so tuition fees are generally measured as a proportion of recurrent costs (which include research and service expenditures) or as a percentage of instructional cost or as a percentage of institutional income. The table uses all of these depending on the availability of data. However, what is included in each of these cost categories may vary from country to country. Therefore, the table paints a picture of financial significance with very broad strokes.

secondary school leaver's family tends to be much higher than GNI per capita would indicate.

Other fees. Some governments and institutions in Africa have implemented fees in higher education but have chosen not to call them "tuition fees" or to identify them with a family- or student-borne share of the underlying costs of instruction. Nevertheless, such fees can effectively supplement government revenue with family- or student-borne contributions. In Nigeria, for example, student contributions are made through a multitude of fees: examination fees, registration fees, hostel maintenance fees, acceptance fees, student union fees, medical registration fees, identity card fees, departmental registration fees, library fees, management information system fees, and late registration fees. In Ghana, significant academic fees were introduced in 2006 that, as of 2009, ranged (depending on program) from ₵258 (US$235) to ₵355 (US$323) per year for continuing undergraduate residents.

In Côte d'Ivoire, the University of Cocody's Faculty of Health recently (February 2009) increased fees by more than 700 percent from CFAF 6,000 (US$21) to CFAF 50,000 (US$174) to the vocal dismay of its students. Other countries, including Cameroon, Burkina Faso, Mauritania, Senegal, and Togo, have also introduced significant student fees.

Government Provision of Student Support Services

Social expenditures represent up to 28 percent of the recurrent budget for higher education (average for 27 African countries, not including social expenditure outside the country; see table 3.6). If money spent outside these countries were included, this share would rise to 41 percent, which is twice as high as in Organisation for Economic Co-operation and Development (OECD) countries (19 percent). However, there are important cross-country differences, as the percentage of social expenditures ranges from 13 percent in Malawi to 70 percent in Guinea-Bissau and Niger (see figure 3.3).

Detailed examination reveals that the relatively lower share of teaching-related expenditure in Africa results from trade-offs in favor of social expenditure at the expense of operational costs. In other words, wages compete directly with social expenditures (see figure 3.4). Accordingly, in many African countries, student-teacher ratios are high because, for a given wage level, channeling a significant share of the budget to social expenditure reduces the capacity to create teaching posts.

Nevertheless, notable change can and does occur. For instance, the share of teaching-related allocations in recurrent expenditure on higher

Table 3.6 Composition of Higher Education Budget, by Country Group, 2006 or Closest Year

Country group	Salaries	Operating costs	Social expenditures In country	Social expenditures Outside country	Total
Africa					
Including grants outside the country	40	19	23	18[a]	100
Not including grants outside the country	49[a]	23[b]	28[c]	n.a.	100
OECD	68	13	n.a.	19	100

Source: Pôle de Dakar 2008.
Note: n.a. = not applicable; OECD = Organisation for Economic Co-operation and Development.
a. Average for 19 countries.
b. Average for 18 countries.
c. Average for 27 countries.

education increased in Côte d'Ivoire in the period 1999–2007 and in Guinea-Bissau in the period 2001–06.[10]

Out-of-country social expenditures represent up to 18 percent of the recurrent higher education budget (average of 19 African, mostly Francophone, countries; see table 3.7). Students from Sub-Saharan Africa are among the most mobile in the world, as statistics of the United Nations Educational, Scientific, and Cultural Organization (UNESCO) show. In 2004, one out of every 16 African students (5.9 percent) studied out-of-country compared to less than one out of every 50 students worldwide (UIS 2006). Nearly three-quarters of African students who study abroad go to Western Europe or North America. Because of the high costs of study in these countries, out-of-country social expenditures quickly become a significant share of the national higher education budget (see box 3.9). This is particularly true not only for small countries such as Guinea-Bissau, Djibouti, or Lesotho, but also for larger ones such as Mauritania or Niger.

As social support policies are becoming increasingly unsustainable, some African countries have started to shift costs from governments to students and families by freezing (particularly in times of high inflation), reducing, or even eliminating student scholarships and other student subsidies. This avoids the politically difficult issue of implementing fees. This trend has been noted in West Africa, where student welfare allowances have declined from a high in 1990.[11] In Burkina Faso, following independence, all students who passed the school-leaving baccalaureate exam automatically benefited from a yearly government grant. However, in

Figure 3.3 Breakdown of Current Public Expenditure on Higher Education in Select African Countries

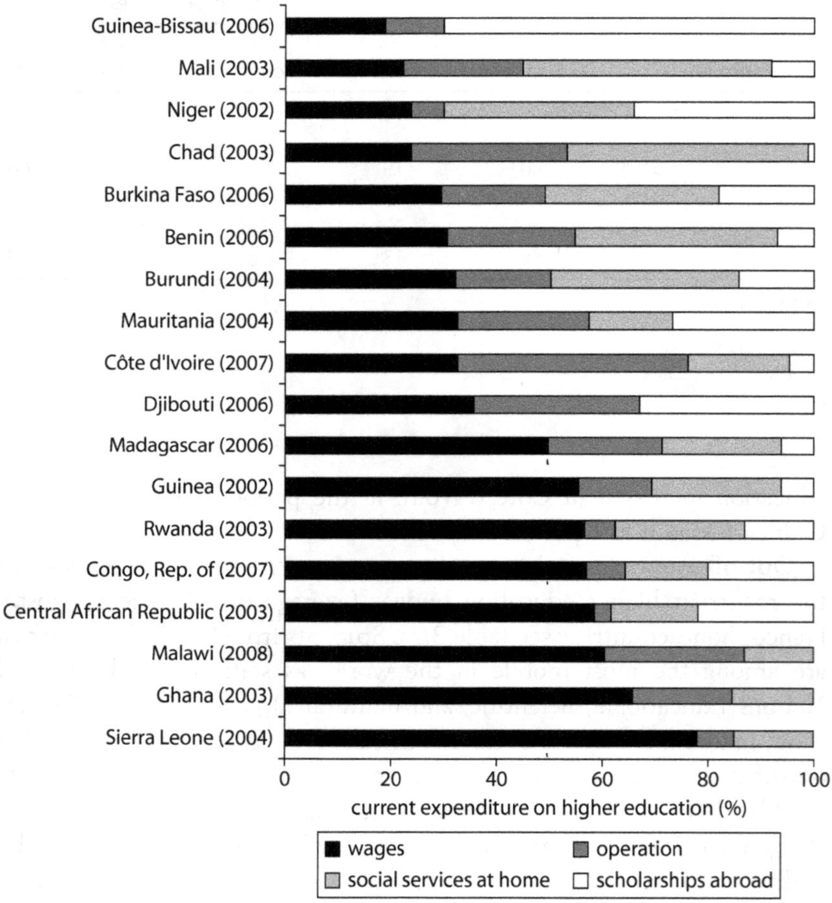

Source: Pôle de Dakar unpublished data.
Note: This graph is limited to 18 countries for which data are available for the four categories of expenditures. For Ghana and Malawi, the share of scholarships abroad is included in country social expenditures.

2001, the government gave only 200 grants. In 1993, the government of Cameroon eliminated its generous scholarship system. Between 1992 and 2000, the government of Côte d'Ivoire froze scholarships and ended free transport services for students.

Some countries have introduced fees for services that had hitherto been free of charge, such as food and housing (sometimes accompanied by the privatization of food and housing services). In Ghana, university

Figure 3.4 Trade-off between Social and Wage Expenditure within the Public Higher Education Budget in Select African Countries

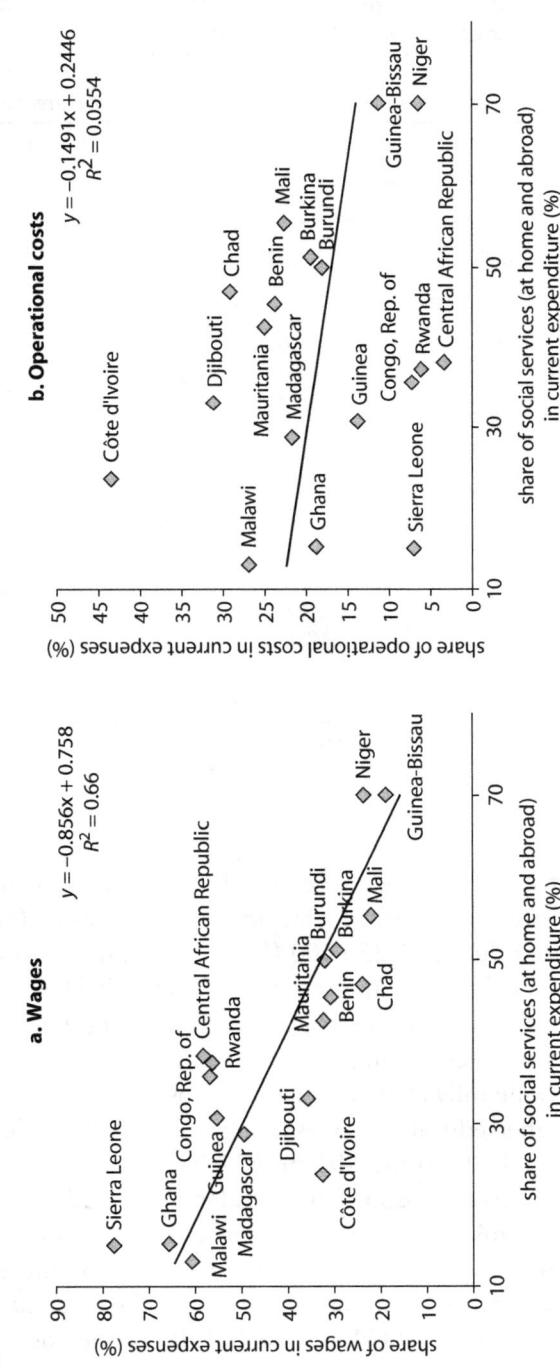

Source: Pôle de Dakar 2008.

Table 3.7 Share of Scholarships Abroad in Current Higher Education Expenditures in 19 African Countries, Most Recent Year Available

Country	Year	Share of scholarships in current expenditures (%)
Benin	2008	6
Burkina Faso	2006	18
Burundi	2008	14
Cameroon	2008	4
Central African Republic	2005	22
Chad	2003	1
Congo, Rep. of	2007	20
Côte d'Ivoire	2007	5
Djibouti	2006	33
Guinea	2005	6
Guinea-Bissau	2006	70
Lesotho	2006	36
Madagascar	2006	7
Mali	2008	2
Mauritania	2007	33
Niger	2002	34
Rwanda	2003	13
Senegal	2007	14
Togo	2007	2
Average 19 countries		18

Sources: Sectoral or subsectoral studies by country; national data; authors' calculations.

residential facility user fees were introduced in 1998. As of 2009, residential students were charged a facility user fee of ₵650,000 (US$359) plus dormitory dues of ₵250,000 (US$138), while nonresidential students paid a small facility user fee of ₵20,000 (US$11).[12] In Tanzania, students became responsible for their own food and housing costs, student union fees, and housing deposit starting in 1993. In 2002, Malawi students became fully responsible for the cost of boarding as part of the country's higher education cost-sharing policy. In Uganda, at a recent meeting (May 3, 2009) the Makerere University Council canceled free meals for government-sponsored students. Instead, starting in the 2009/10 academic year, these students will receive a daily meal allowance of U sh 2,000. The council has directed the university to invite private companies to run restaurants for the students. In countries such as Senegal (late 1990s) and Benin (2004), the cost of meals was increased for the first time in many years.

Box 3.9

The Cost of Studies Abroad: The Case of Mauritius

In 2007 in Mauritius, the number of students abroad corresponded to one-third of all in-country students. These studies cost about half of the total financing for higher education within Mauritius. In this context, public resources amounted to only one-quarter of the funding for higher education (see table below).

Box Table Allocation of Higher Education Financing in Mauritius, by Source, Destination, and Unit Cost, 2007

Destination and source	Percentage of total financing	Number of students in 2007	Cost per student (US$ 2007)
Public institutions in Mauritius	25.40	15,463	2,423
Public source	21.50	—	2,048
Private source	3.90	—	375
Private institutions in Mauritius	20.00	9,293	3,167
Institutions abroad	54.60	8,473	9,500
Total	100.00	33,229	4,435

Source: SARUA 2009.
Note: — = not available.

Development of the Private Higher Education Sector

Private higher education has experienced spectacular growth in Africa. In 2006, it accounted for 22 percent of higher education students on the continent, a percentage close to levels observed in Europe (a 13-country average of 28 percent), but considerably lower than Latin American levels (approximately 50 percent).[13] This expansion occurred in response to excess and differentiated social demand (Varghese 2004). Although insufficient capacity, quality problems, and inadequate management of public institutions may in certain countries contribute to the development of the private sector, no such impact assessments have been carried out. Generally speaking, private higher education institutions endeavor to grow by offering training courses that are different from those available in the public sector and by organizing short vocational courses in disciplines requiring limited technological equipment to keep prices attractive. The appeal of such institutions depends largely on their capacity to adapt and respond to labor market needs and trends, thereby enhancing students' employability.

Private higher education is developing in most African countries, but its share varies extensively from country to country (see figure 3.5). In Cape Verde, a private university was established in 2001, well before the creation of a public university in 2005. Conversely, private higher education in Mauritania was authorized recently by a law adopted in 2008. In any case, the implementation of a regulatory framework and incentive measures as, for instance, in Côte d'Ivoire, clearly has had a positive impact on the development of the private sector.

Diversification of Financing Sources

The autonomy of higher education institutions enables them to mobilize additional private funds, which are rarely accounted for and may be considerable. Greater transparency in identifying and managing such supplementary resources would allow the state to improve the resource allocation system as a whole and to streamline its management.

On average, own resources account for approximately 28 percent of the revenue of higher education public institutions in the 13 countries for which data are available (see table 3.8). The share of own resources is lowest (5 percent or less) in Madagascar and Zimbabwe and highest in Guinea-Bissau (75 percent) and Uganda (56 percent). Institutions may generate considerable own resources even in countries offering free higher education. Benin's two public universities, where fee-based vocational training courses generate approximately 40 percent of their operating budget (excluding salaries), are a case in point. The coexistence of free academic instruction and fee-charging vocational training carries the risk of skewing the system toward free but underfinanced disciplines, which already absorb more than 80 percent of student enrollment. To reduce that risk, Benin has adopted a mechanism for distributing the supplementary resources in question among various common services within the university and indirectly channeling some of the profit to the programs offered free of charge. These supplementary resources should ideally augment effective public expenditure per student and be directed toward improving quality. To date, however, they have been limited to mitigating the decline in quality during the last decade.

Student Financial Assistance

The introduction of cost sharing without financial assistance would exacerbate existing disparities between the well-off and the much larger numbers of the poor, between urban and rural populations, and in many countries between dominant ethnic and linguistic groups and marginalized

Figure 3.5 Proportion of African Students Enrolled in Private Institutions, 35 Countries, 2006 (or Closest Year)

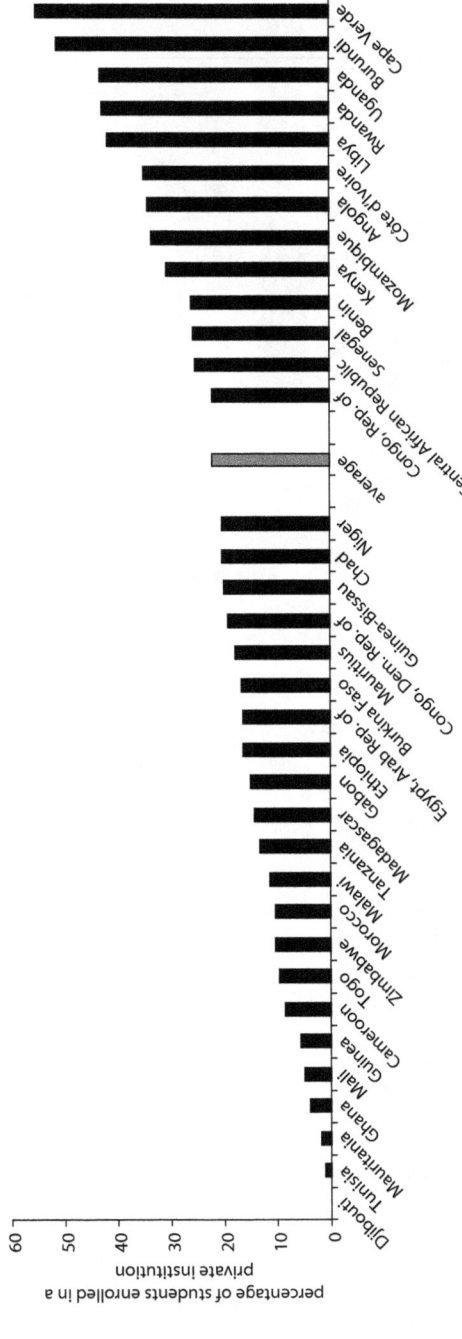

Source: National and UIS data.
Note: grey column represents the average.

Table 3.8 Share of Own Resources in the Total Revenue of Public Higher Education Institutions in Select African Countries

Country or public institution	Share of total revenue (%)
Benin, 2008	23[a]
Ghana, 2003	37
Guinea-Bissau, 2006	75
Amilcar Cabral University	88
Medical School	65
Law School	36
Kenya, 2007	39
Madagascar, 2006	3
Malawi	22
University of Malawi, 2008	22
Bunda College of Agriculture	12
Chancellor College	14
College of Medicine	50
Kamuzu College of Nursing	13
Malawi Polytechnic	20
University Central Office	6
Mzuni University, 2005	27
Mauritius, 2007	15
Namibia, 2002	32
University of Namibia	29
Polytechnic	37
Senegal, 2007	
Cheikh Anta Diop University	21[a]
Swaziland, 2007	20
Tanzania, 2006	18
Moshi University College of Cooperative and Business Studies	30
Open University	34
University College of Lands and Architectural Studies	25
Sokoine University of Agriculture	17
University of Dar es Salaam	11
Muhimbili College University of Health Sciences	9
Mzumbe University	29
Dar es Salaam Institute of Technology	32
State University of Zanzibar	8
Uganda, 2006	56
University of Makerere	60
Mbara University of Science and Technology	22
Kyambogo University	51
Zimbabwe	5
Average	28

Sources: SARUA 2009, sector and subsector studies, national data, and authors' calculations.
a. Calculated on the basis of total Ministry of Higher Education expenditure.

groups (including, in some countries, women). In short, cost sharing can bring new resources to higher education to expand capacity, improve quality, and even expand accessibility and equity. But it can accomplish these things only (a) if governments continue their current support for higher education, using the potential new revenue from families and students to supplement rather than supplant or substitute for what in most African countries are still rather generous, even if declining, government contributions and (b) if financial assistance continues to be provided in the forms of means-tested grants based on parental income and student loans.

Financial assistance policies are therefore critical components of cost-sharing policies in Africa. In the countries that have begun to introduce tuition and other fees and to charge for room and board, a variety of accompanying grant and loan programs have been developed. Table 3.9 outlines the main student financial assistance programs and their reach in select countries. One of the main distinctions is between those financial aid programs that are means tested, those that are allocated based on some other criteria such as merit, and those that are available to all students. It is mainly in the Francophone countries (with some exceptions) that all students receive financial assistance in the form of no tuition fees coupled with grants for living expenses (see table 3.9).

Loan Programs

The concept of student loans has existed in Africa for more than 50 years, with loan programs having been proposed as early as 1952 in Lesotho and 1966 in Botswana. The first full-fledged loan programs were introduced in Nigeria in 1973 and Kenya in 1974 (Woodhall 1991). As of 2008, at least 13 African countries have operational loan programs, and several more are considering establishing programs (Burundi, Mauritius, Mozambique, and Uganda).[14] The success of these loans must be measured not only by whether they meet their specific program objectives, but also by whether they are financially sustainable, as without sustainability the program will not survive, whatever its objectives (Ziderman 2004). A loan's political acceptability is also critical for its long-term survival.

Objectives

In response to the cost-sharing imperative and the introduction of tuition fees, recent loan programs have been created in Africa to allow students and their families to share in the costs of higher education by covering tuition fees and maintenance costs. As in the rest of the world, student

Table 3.9 Student Financial Assistance Programs in African Countries

Country	Student aid program and description	Significance of financial assistance
Angola	Government grants for living costs	3,000 in 2009
Benin	Government grants, grants, and financial aid range from €45 to €80 per month; most, but not all, grant holders also receive subsidized housing.	In 2006/07, 8,733 students received government grants based on merit and age (17% of students) and 8,393 received financial aid (15% of students) based on merit and age.
Botswana	Grant-loan scheme	Tertiary Education Development Fund and the Department of Student Placement and Welfare sponsored 26,943 tertiary students in 2004 (it is not clear whether this refers to a grant-loan scheme or additional sponsorship).
Burkina Faso	Merit-based grants (CFAF 500,000 per year); FONER loans (financial aid for students who do not receive merit-based state grants) started in 1992; financial aid is CFAF 150,000 (US$749) per year, renewable twice (students cannot receive both a loan and aid); the amount of the loan is CFAF 200,000 per year.	In 2007/08, 2,233 students received a grant, 21,620 received financial aid, and 3,862 received a loan.
Burundi	Students receive little direct financial assistance (FBu 370 per year).	In 2007/08, the number of students who received a grant was 9,904 in the public sector (46%) and 2,861 in the private sector (25%).
Cameroon	Financial assistance is based on need and merit (also financial assistance for girls studying science fields).	In 2007, financial aid was given to 442 students (out of 108,000 higher education students).
Central African Republic	Government grants	No information
Chad	Government grants	2,995 grant holders (out of 8,000 students in 2003)

Congo, Democratic Rep. of	Students receive little direct financial assistance.	None
Congo, Rep. of	Government grants for all qualified students	No information
Côte d'Ivoire	Government grants for all qualified students	16,500 grant holders studying in-country (about 10% of students)
Ethiopia	Deferred tuition fees and deferred maintenance costs for all qualified students	Close to 100% of all students
Gabon	Government grants (provision of living allowances) for all qualified students	Most students
Ghana	Student loans	No information
Guinea	State grants (monthly student stipends) for all qualified students	No information
Kenya	In addition to means-tested loans, needy students also receive means-tested financial aid; the maximum amount per year that a student can receive in grants is K Sh 8,000 (US$107); students in both private and public universities can also apply for grants or scholarships from the Constituency Development Fund.	50,000 university students benefited from HELB loans and grants in 2007/08.
Lesotho	Loan grant; the amount that has to be paid back is contingent on successful completion of degree and employment in the Lesotho civil service.	No information
Madagascar	Government grants for all qualified students	82% of students receive grants.
Malawi	Grants and loans for fees	30% of undergraduates receive grants or loans.
Mali	National grants based on results and age	In 2007/08, about 33,000 students received a grant or a half grant (depending on results and age); the average of the grant and half grant was CFAF 230,000 a year.
Mauritania	Socially targeted stipends	In 2006/07, 4,201 students (36%) received a grant and 2,438 (21%) received financial aid; the average per student was UM 106,000.

(continued)

Table 3.9 Student Financial Assistance Programs in African Countries *(continued)*

Country	Student aid program and description	Significance of financial assistance
Mauritius	Means-tested grants covering cost of tuition fees, books, exam fees, and living costs; up to MUR 150,000 a year (US$10,217) was from the newly established (2008) Human Resources, Knowledge, and Arts Development Fund.	No information
Mozambique	Grants (full and partial) given by public higher education institutions to students based on eligibility criteria and procedures (part of public direct financing to institutions); provincial scholarships	About 10% of students in public higher education institutions receive grants or live in subsidized housing and receive assistance to purchase books.
Namibia	Means-tested Student Financial Assistance Scheme: in 2003/04, more than N$48 million (US$11.2 million) was allocated to student support.	In 2002, 40% of University of Namibia students received some kind of financial support.
Nigeria	Needs-based financial assistance (₦25,000 in 2002) and student loans	In 2002, 40,000 students received financial assistance.
Rwanda	SFAR student loans (means tested); merit-based SFAR grants cover the cost of studies and living costs for students who have received a "distinction" grade in select S&T majors or "higher distinction" in other courses.	During the 2008 academic year, 15,710 students benefited from SFAR grants and loans (about 60% of public and private higher education students).
Senegal	A generous grants policy covers both fees and living costs based on academic merit; full grant: CFAF 36,000 (US$143); two-thirds grant: CFAF 24,000 (US$95); and half grant: CFAF 18,000 (US$72).	No information

South Africa	It is possible, depending on a student's academic results, to have up to 40% of the National Student Financial Aid Scheme of South Africa loan converted to a grant (Jackson 2002)	About 15% of undergraduates in public institutions receive loans.
Swaziland	Grants and loans	95% of all students receive some type of financial support (grants and loans).
Tanzania	Means-tested deferred tuition fees and deferred maintenance costs	In 2007/08, 55,981 loans were made out of 68,001 loan applications.
Uganda	Government-sponsored students receive free tuition, room, and board	About one-quarter of all students in public universities
Zambia	Grants for up to 75% of total costs (fees, books, living expenses)	For 7,500 students per year
Zimbabwe	Cadetship scheme whereby very needy students receive financial support but are required to work in the public sector for a fixed number of years following graduation	No information

Source: Authors.

Note: In this table, *bourse* is translated as *grant* (generally merit based) and *aide* is translated as *financial assistance* or *aid* (generally need based). *Bursary* is synonymous with *grant*. FONER = Fond National pour l'Education et la Recherche; HELB = Higher Education Loans Board; SFAR = Student Financing Agency for Rwanda.

loan programs are being created as part of larger cost-sharing policies to meet the twin and somewhat competing goals of increasing university revenue from nongovernment sources and expanding access to traditionally underserved populations. Given the low incomes prevailing in Africa, effective implementation of cost sharing or revenue supplementation almost always requires some form of student lending to succeed.

The loan programs have both cost-sharing and access-participation objectives. A few of them have additional objectives. For example, in an effort to improve student completion rates, the National Student Financial Scheme of South Africa converts 40 percent of the loan to a grant if the borrower performs well academically (Jackson 2002). In Botswana, the scheme is explicitly designed to influence program selection in addition to its other objectives. All students are eligible for the grant-loan scheme, but the portion of their tuition fees and maintenance costs that they are required to pay back depends on what they study. The Lesotho National Manpower Development Secretariat Loan Bursaries Scheme aims to influence postgraduation behavior in addition to its other objectives. It requires graduates who leave the country to pay back 100 percent of their tuition fees and living expenses.

Depending on the objectives set, student loans in Africa have been designed differently. The main design parameters include interest rate, coverage eligibility, whether they are means tested, whether they cover all the costs, the repayment period and criteria, whether the program has deferment and forbearance options, repayment obligations, and modalities including whether they are income contingent or not, and, finally, the legal enforcement framework. Table 3.10 summarizes the characteristics of the existing student loan programs in Africa.

Financial Sustainability

In general, the record of student loan recovery in Sub-Saharan Africa is exceedingly poor (see table 3.11). Cost recovery depends on (a) program design, mainly an interest rate that can recover all or most of the initial cost, and (b) successful and cost-effective collection. In other words, the interest rate may be sufficient (for example, only minimally subsidized), but if students are not aware that the loans carry a repayment obligation or if little effort is made to reach and collect from the borrowers or if the law does not support debt collection, the default rate will be unacceptably high. Likewise, the loan administration and collections systems may be fully computerized and run by trained staff, but if the loans carry a low interest rate and feature long repayment periods, cost recovery will be very low.

Table 3.10 Student Loan Schemes in Africa

Country and scheme	Coverage and eligibility	Loan parameters (interest rate, grace period, and repayment)	Range of borrowing	Number of students borrowing
Botswana				
Grant-loan scheme administered by Department of Student Placement and Welfare (DSPW), introduced in 1995	Students in public and private sector (as of 2007) institutions; tuition fees and maintenance costs; local and external tertiary programs; awarded based on national priority accorded to the course of study	Interest free; three-month grace period after obtaining employment; upon graduation, borrowers to notify DSPW, which informs them of the exact amount they owe	The extent to which their grant needs to be paid back dependent on what they study (five categories): category 1 students (studying subjects that need human resources): 100% grant for both tuition fees and maintenance costs; category 2 students: 100% grant for tuition fees but have to repay 50% of maintenance; category 3 students: have to repay 50% of tuition fee costs and 100% of maintenance costs	Between 1995 and 2001, close to 5,000 borrowed money under the scheme.
Burkina Faso				
FONER loans, introduced in 1994	Students in public sector institutions (third-year students and up); maintenance costs; means tested	3% interest from loan origination; one-year grace period; income-contingent repayment at one-sixteenth of salary; repayment period of six years	CFAF 200,000 (US$998) starting in 2007/08 academic year, of which CFAF 15,000 a year (US$75) is allocated to fees	Since 1994, more than 36,639 loans have been paid out, totaling CFAF 5.851 billion.

(continued)

Table 3.10 Student Loan Schemes in Africa *(continued)*

Country and scheme	Coverage and eligibility	Loan parameters (interest rate, grace period, and repayment)	Range of borrowing	Number of students borrowing
Ethiopia				
Graduate tax,[a] introduced in 2003	Students in public sector institutions; full cost of meals, housing, health services, and student portion of instructional costs; all enrolled students	Simple interest calculated on total amount owed; interest rate used: average of bank rates while the student is in school; grace period of one year after graduation; income-contingent repayment of at least 10% of monthly income; maximum repayment period of 15 years	Br 3,625–Br 5,871 (US$1,290–US$1,814) a year (2008/09)	Close to 100% of public sector students have borrowed.
Ghana				
Students Loan Trust Fund, introduced in 2006/07 academic year[b]	Students in public and private sector institutions; living expenses; means tested	During study and grace period, interest rate equal to prevailing 182-day Government of Ghana Treasury Bill (in 2007: 10.25%) compounded annually; during repayment period, interest rate equal to the prevailing 182-day Treasury Bill plus 4%	Amount based on needs of each student, that is, the difference between the full cost of study and estimated family contribution	Since 2005, 5,000 students have received loans.

		compounded semiannually; grace period of one year following completion; repayment via monthly deductions from a borrower's salary by the employer or via direct periodic payments by a borrower who is self-employed; 15-year repayment period	
Kenya			
HELB, introduced in 1995	Students in public and private sector institutions; tuition and maintenance; means tested	4% interest compounded starting from loan origination; one-year grace period following program completion; conventional repayment though repayments possibly deducted by employer and remitted to board; loan repayments not to exceed one-quarter of borrower's monthly salary	Maximum: K Sh 60,000 (US$2,032) In 2006/07, 28,900 were awarded loans.
Lesotho			
National Manpower Development Secretariat loan grant scheme, introduced in 1978	Students in public sector institutions; tuition fees and living expenses	No interest; no grace period; repayment expected within five years in equal monthly installments	Workers in the public service required to pay back 50% of loan, workers in the private sector required	In 2003/04, 8,593 were supported; in 2003/04, 5,247 students in the National University of Lesotho were

(continued)

Table 3.10 Student Loan Schemes in Africa *(continued)*

Country and scheme	Coverage and eligibility	Loan parameters (interest rate, grace period, and repayment)	Range of borrowing	Number of students borrowing
			to pay back 65%, and workers outside of Lesotho required to pay back 100%	provided with National Manpower Development Secretariat scholarships out of a total of 7,000 students.
Malawi				
University Students Loan Scheme	Students in public sector institutions; student fees; means tested	No interest; grace period for six months after obtaining employment; maximum repayment period of 10 years	MK 25,000 (US$633) per year	No information
Namibia				
Namibia Student Financial Assistance Fund, created in 1997	Students in public sector institutions; tuition fees, textbooks, registration fees, and related educational expenses; loans for living expenses only in cases of exceptional need; allocated according to regional quotas and field of study priorities; means tested	Interest equal to half of the prime rate; grace period during in-school years (no interest compounded) and six months after study completion, if student has found employment and is earning threshold salary (N$R17 a week); income-contingent repayments of up to 15% of borrower's salary; short repayment horizon	Maximum of N$R15,000 (US$3,520) for engineering students	On average, 4,000 per year; 22,000 students borrowed between 1997 and 2006, with total amount of N$R400 per student.

Scheme	Eligibility	Terms	Loan amount	Coverage
Nigeria Education Tax Fund and the Student's Scholarship Board consolidated into Education Trust Fund in 2007	Students in public and private sector institutions; fees and approved living expenses; means tested	7% interest; grace period of up to two years after graduation (not clear if interest is compounded during this time) or until employment obtained (whichever comes first); maximum repayment period of 10 years (length of repayment period designated as three times the number of years the student was in receipt of the loan)	No information	No information
Rwanda Student Financing Agency for Rwanda (SFAR) student loan scheme, set up in 2003; 2007 law made it an independent entity	Students in accredited higher education institutions; tuition and maintenance; from 2008, means tested and students to meet academic requirements	5% interest; grace period while in school and one year after graduation (interest compounded from loan origination); income-contingent repayment; employers required to deduct loan payments from salaries on a monthly basis (8% of gross salary)	RF 1.2 million to RF 1.5 million (US$6,445 to US$8,057)	About 60% of higher education students receive SFAR loans and grants; 22,000 former and current university students owe repayments.
South Africa National Student Financial Aid Scheme, 1999	Students in public sector institutions; tuition or maintenance; means tested	Interest rate: varies at rate of inflation plus an additional 2% to cover administrative	R 2,000 to R 32,500 (US$516 to US$8,397) in 2006	20% of student population

(continued)

Table 3.10 Student Loan Schemes in Africa *(continued)*

Country and scheme	Coverage and eligibility	Loan parameters (interest rate, grace period, and repayment)	Range of borrowing	Number of students borrowing
		and long-term unemployment and default costs; interest compounded from loan origination and accrued even during times of unemployment or when salary is below the repayment threshold; grace period until borrower is employed; repayments by borrower on income-contingent basis when salary reaches R 30,000; maximum repayment rate 8% of income, but starts at 3% and increases 1% for every R 6,600 above that; no maximum repayment period		
Swaziland				
Loan component of scholarship under the Scholarship Secretariat	Students in public sector institutions; tuition and other fees	5% simple interest once payment begins; grace period until employment is obtained; payment of	Loan component of the scholarship	All government-sponsored students (local students not sponsored by their employers or international students)

	of Ministry of Education		50% of total amount received from government; repayment period of four to eight years	
Tanzania				
HESLB, introduced in July 2005, replacing older scheme that was established in 1994	Students in public (with the exception of fee-paying students) and private institutions; tuition fees, other academic fees, room and board; means tested; full-time students only	No interest; grace period of one year after completion; repayments deducted from borrower's salary (agrees with the board on amount to be deducted; borrower may also pay in equal monthly installments; maximum repayment period of 10–15 years	Amount of loan awarded to each student dependent on means-testing results as well as the upper loan limit for each item; means-testing results categorized as A (100%), B (80%), C (60%), D (40%), E (20%), and F (0%)	In 2007, 5,628 students received loans amounting to T Sh 99.2 billion (US$250,739,000); in 2008/09, government committed to disbursing T Sh 117 billion (about US$250.7 million) to 48,684 students (85,000 students in higher education in Tanzania, that is, more than 50%); in 2008/09, 2,652 first-year students received loans covering 100% of costs; 10,917 first-year students received loans covering 80% of costs, 500 first-year students received loans for lesser amounts; 36,729 continuing students received loans.

Sources: Authors' calculations; Adongo 2008; Cheboi 2008; Cheboi and Jackson 2008; International Comparative Higher Education Finance and Accessibility 2008; Musisi 2007; Pillay 2008, 2009; Sayed and others 2008; Siphambe 2008; Some 2006; World Bank 2007b.

Note: FONER = Fond National pour l'Education et la Recherche; HELB = Higher Education Loans Board; HESLB = Higher Education Students Loans Board; SFAR = Student Financing Agency for Rwanda.

a. The Ethiopian graduate tax is actually an income-contingent loan. Students and families are given a 5 percent discount for up-front payment and a 3 percent discount for payment within the first year after graduation.

b. Those students who started with the Social Security and National Insurance Trust scheme will continue with that scheme.

Table 3.11 Loan Recovery in Select African Countries

Country	Loan recovery
Botswana	As of 2009, only P 20 million had been collected out of more than P 4 billion loaned by the ministry over the past 15 years. The scheme is scheduled for review because of minimal collection and other problems.
Burkina Faso	As of 2003, out of the 9,917 beneficiaries of FONER (loans and grants), 7,189 borrowers are in arrears, and bad debts amount to CFAF 818,270,000 plus CFAF 24,548,1000 in interest. Some recovery has started from public sector employees. Only CFAF 6 million–CFAF 10 million has been recovered.
Ethiopia	Yearly collections by the Inland Revenue and Customs Authority totaled Br 516,039 in 2006/07; Br 1,240,115 in 2007/08; and Br 2,420,310 in 2008/09.
Kenya	26,720 graduates have fully repaid their loans. Another 57,000 have not yet begun servicing their loans.
Lesotho	The recovery rate is so low that loans are essentially a grant. There has been no recovery of loans thus far, but plans are under way.
Namibia	Loan recovery was very low until 2006. 10,478 students owe money, and of these, 1,153 are paying back their loans, while the rest are unemployed, have extended their loans, or are studying further or their files are at the Attorney General's Office.
Rwanda	Until recently (2007) no loan recovery mechanisms were in place. RF 1.5 million was collected during official launching ceremony in November 2007. SFAR recovered RF 463,400 million in 2008 out of RF 15 billion owed.
South Africa	Given that 40 percent of the loan is converted to a grant if academic performance is good, recovery per se is not a good measure of success. R 204.8 million was recovered between 1998 and 2006.
Swaziland	As of 2006, E 289 million was owed.
Tanzania	Currently the debt owed by 113,240 students who borrowed between 1994 and 2005 stands at T Sh 51.1 billion (T Sh 20.7 billion of which is due for repayment). HESLB has recovered T Sh 776.6 million from 9,424 borrowers, but has traced only 10,701 of the students who owe money.

Source: Authors' calculations.
Note: FONER = Fond National pour l'Education et la Recherche; HESLB = Higher Education Loans Board; SFAR = Student Financing Agency for Rwanda.

The following patterns explain the failure in recovering payment and ensuring the financial sustainability of student loans.

One, *inadequate means testing allows students to borrow who have no real financial need.* Most of the loan programs in Africa are "generally available," which means that their allocation is not predicated on the financial soundness of a student and his or her family but is made available in some cases to all students and is targeted in others to students who are needy, from certain underprivileged regions, or in certain academic fields. Nine of the 13 loan programs in Africa use means testing in the awarding of loans, while in Ethiopia, Lesotho, and Swaziland, loans are available to all higher education students. Meanwhile, in Botswana the award is based on the priority accorded to the course. Means testing has been criticized for not targeting truly needy students. Some countries such as Tanzania have improved their data collection to have a more accurate assessment of the socioeconomic situation of applicants and their families.

Two, *interest rates are set far too low (generally by politicians fearful of student resistance to cost sharing, which is often associated with student loans)*. Four of the loan programs charge no interest (Botswana, Lesotho, Malawi, and Tanzania, although the Higher Education Students Loans Board [HESLB], in Tanzania is working to change this); of the other nine that do charge interest, only three (Ghana, South Africa, and Ethiopia) charge a real interest rate (that is, greater than the prevailing rate of inflation), and only four (Ghana, Kenya,[15] Rwanda, and South Africa) compound interest during the in-school years and grace period. This means that, in more than half of the programs, significant interest subsidies are built into the program, which has a negative impact on cost recovery.

Three, *grace periods and repayment periods are unnecessarily long and exacerbate the losses from the excessive subsidization of interest*. Repayment periods in African student loan programs range from very short, as in Lesotho and Namibia, to indefinite, as in South Africa (Shen and Ziderman 2007). When loans carry a subsidized interest rate, as the majority of those in Africa do, these varying payment periods have implications for the size of the grant that is hidden inside the loan.

Four, *loans are disbursed in such a way that students are frequently unaware that they are incurring a real repayment obligation*. Loans in Africa are mainly disbursed directly to the higher education institute to cover tuition fees and to the student to cover living costs. However, in countries with fully deferred tuition fees, such as Botswana, Ethiopia, and Lesotho, students never see any of the money, which may limit their understanding of their repayment obligations. In Tanzania, the HESLB pays tuition fees directly to the higher education institution but requires that the student borrower acknowledge receipt of these funds by signing a copy of the payment list issued by the board. While disbursing loans directly to the institutions may make the concept of the loan less real to students, it also removes the risk that students will use the funds for purposes other than education.

Five, *many of the student loan programs in Africa forgive all or part of the loan under certain conditions*. A loan may be forgiven if a student successfully completes his or her program, studies in a certain field, or lives or works in a certain location after graduation. In Ethiopia, teachers and other professionals deemed to be of public interest are exempt from paying the so-called graduate tax. In Lesotho, those who work in the public sector are required to pay back only 50 percent of the loan, those who work in the private sector are required to pay back 65 percent of the loan, and those who work outside Lesotho are required to repay 100 percent of the loan. In Botswana, students who studied on programs for which there is a shortage of personnel in the country receive forgiveness of all the tuition fees and maintenance costs they owe.

Six, *legal systems make debt collection expensive and frequently unsuccessful.* Regarding legal enforcement, some student loan programs in Africa, including Kenya, Ghana, Tanzania, and Rwanda, were established with weak or nonexistent enabling legislation, and it was only when semiautonomous boards were established with real enforcement powers for collecting loans or for requiring employers to collect loans that real cost recovery began. The critical role of legislation is highlighted in the case of the Fond National pour l'Education et la Recherche (FONER) loans in Burkina Faso. One of the weaknesses of these loans is the lack of legal provision for recovery. Even when debtors are tracked down, there is no legal recourse to force them to repay, and the government does not have the legal power to require employers to deduct repayments from the borrowers' wages (Some 2006).

Seven, *the timing and size of a loan can have negative implications for its repayment.* Loans disbursed too late in the semester do not help students to cover their up-front costs. In Ghana, under a program of the Social Security and National Insurance Trust, students had to start the school year before turning in their loan application and therefore did not receive funds until well into the semester. By contrast, the Student Loan Trust Fund (SLTF) instead has the students complete loan applications at the same time as they apply for admission to a higher education institution so that the loans can be disbursed at the beginning of the semester when students need them to pay their fees.

Eight, *the adequacy of student loans to cover all costs is an important factor in their recovery.* If loans are not large enough to cover all costs, this may discourage students from low socioeconomic backgrounds from attending at all. Inadequate loans may also lead students to live in substandard conditions or not get enough to eat and ultimately to drop out and have a difficult time finding employment. It is significantly more difficult to collect from unemployed borrowers. In Burkina Faso, for example, students complain that the maximum loan is inadequate to meet university fees and living expenses. Similarly, in Kenya, loan amounts may be adequate for government-sponsored students, but they are not adequate to cover all costs for self-financed students.

Nine, *underdeveloped administrative systems and inadequate staffing do not allow the system to recover significant repayment*. In many of the loan programs in Africa, overworked government bureaucracies are expected to run the student loan schemes in addition to their other work, and they face inadequate staffing, resources, and consultation procedures with other stakeholders. Loan programs appear to work better when specialized government agencies such as the Student Financing Agency for Rwanda (SFAR), the HESLB in Tanzania, the SLTF in Ghana, and the Higher Education Loans Board (HELB) in Kenya administer them and have formal relationships with other stakeholder institutions. While a separate loan agency was not created for the Ethiopia graduate tax, a well-codified set of administrative procedures divides specific administrative responsibilities among the Ministry of Education, the Federal Inland Revenue Authority, and the academic institutions. Campus loan offices have been created in some countries such as Ghana and South Africa to interact directly with students.

Ten, *record keeping cannot adequately track borrowers*. The collection records of student loan programs in Africa have been fairly dismal, and in some countries virtually no repayments have been collected. Nevertheless, this is changing for the better as governments recognize the importance of clear and robust collection systems. In Botswana, the Loans Recovery Service Division was recently created, and the ministry is planning to begin outsourcing student loan collection. The loan programs in Lesotho and Tanzania have also begun to use professional debt collection agencies to raise annual collection rates of outstanding repayments. Some loan program bureaucracies have started to coordinate with other agencies inside and outside of the government. In Ethiopia, the Federal Inland Revenue Authority, the academic institutions, and employers play a role in loan collection under the oversight of the Ministry of Education. In Kenya, HELB works with the credit bureau and the government tax authority to encourage compliance and track down defaulters. It also shares information with the National Social Security Fund and the Government Computer Center. Loan programs are increasingly recognizing that enforceable negative consequences for nonrepayment based in law are critical for collection. In 2008, for example, the Ministry of Education in Namibia reported a 50 percent increase in loan repayment compared to 2006 because, starting that year, the Ministry of Education was allowed to obtain delinquent borrower's employment details from the Social Security Commission.

Eleven, *economies provide too few jobs for the number of college and university graduates.* Many of the loan programs have deferment and forbearance options[16] for borrowers who are having problems repaying due to unemployment or other economic hardships. The HELB student loan program in Kenya, the grant-loan scheme in Botswana, the National Student Financial Aid Scheme in Namibia, and the SFAR program in Rwanda all have explicit deferment options. In, Namibia, for example, a borrower who is unable to find employment within six months of completing his or her course can apply for a repayment extension. Moreover, a borrower who finds employment but is not earning a threshold salary may opt to pay back the loan without interest. Repayments may be suspended if the borrower becomes unemployed, has a salary that falls below the relevant threshold, or becomes disabled and unable to work. When the loan is suspended, no interest is accrued, although it begins to accrue again when repayment resumes. Other loan programs have limited deferment and forbearance options, which may push unemployed students into default. In Botswana, for example, borrowers need to go through a formal assessment to get a 12-month deferral. Ghana, Kenya, Lesotho, Malawi, Nigeria, and Tanzania all have fixed-schedule repayment obligations, while Burkina Faso, Ethiopia, Namibia, Rwanda, and South Africa have income-contingent repayment obligations.

External Assistance to Higher Education

Over the period 2002–06, external donors allocated about US$600 million annually to higher education in Sub-Saharan Africa. However, less than 30 percent of this amount directly benefited African universities. Most of the balance never made it to Sub-Saharan Africa since it was primarily spent in donors' universities to compensate them for the cost of educating African students. This imbalance in aid to higher education certainly limits its impact and makes its current allocation questionable. Donors need to ensure that the share of aid that directly supports the development of higher education systems in Sub-Saharan Africa increases significantly. Clear national strategies in favor of higher education would certainly increase the likelihood of this happening.

Overview of Aid to Higher Education

Between 2002 and 2006, Sub-Saharan Africa was the second largest recipient of aid to higher education. National resources are not alone in supporting the large number of mobile African students, as international aid is also an important source of financing. Over the period 2002–06, external donors allocated an average US$3.3 billion each year to higher education worldwide. Of this, 18 percent, or about US$600 million, was allocated to Sub-Saharan African countries (see figure 3.6). Most bilateral and multilateral donors contributed to financing higher education in Africa. The largest donor was France, with more than US$300 million allocated annually during 2002–06, followed by Germany (US$95 million), Portugal (US$37 million), the International Development Association (US$34 million), Belgium (US$25 million), the Netherlands (US$21 million), the United Kingdom (US$17 million), Norway (US$16 million), and the European Commission (US$11 million).

Resource allocations to higher education are much lower than those to basic education. Over the period 2002–06, aid to basic education in Sub-Saharan African countries was above US$1.1 billion annually (see figure 3.7). This was about twice the amount allocated to higher education. However, the ratio of aid to basic education to aid to higher education varied significantly across countries, from 0.016 in Botswana to 30 in Togo, two countries that have comparable primary net enrollment ratios. It would seem legitimate to target basic education in countries that are far behind in reaching universal primary education and to shift aid as the country's education system develops. However, the absence of correlation

Figure 3.6 Distribution of Aid to Higher Education, by Region, 2002–06 Average (Commitments)

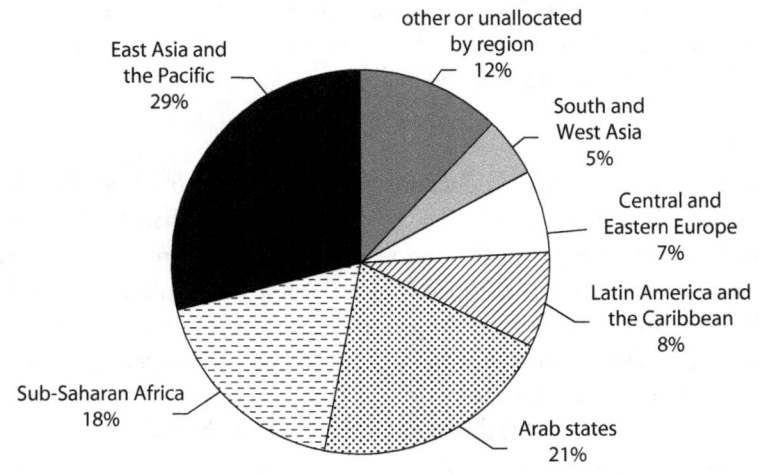

Source: OECD 2009.

Figure 3.7 Aid to Education in Sub-Saharan Africa, by Level of Education, 2002–06 Average

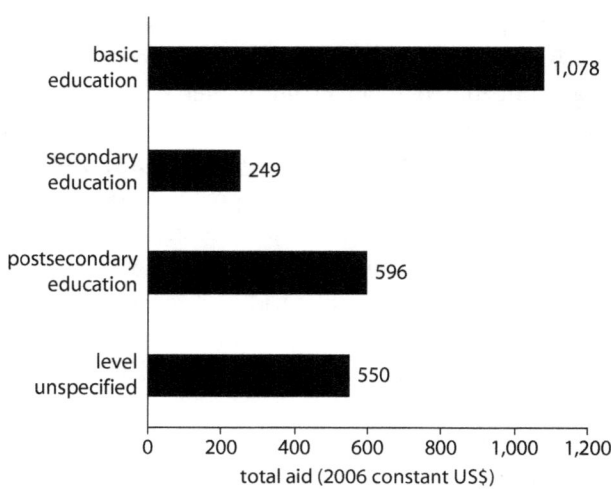

Source: OECD 2009.

between enrollment ratios and share of aid going to basic education reveals a lack of strategy regarding the allocation of aid.

Less than a third of all aid to higher education allocated to Sub-Saharan Africa directly benefited universities and research centers in the region. Figure 3.8 shows the total amounts of aid to higher education to Africa for the period 2002–06 and distinguishes direct from indirect aid (see box 3.10 for the definition of direct and indirect support to higher education). Over the period considered, direct aid to African higher education systems averaged US$152 million annually, or 26 percent of the total, and indirect aid absorbed the remaining US$444 million.

Direct External Aid

Direct support to higher education is evenly distributed across African countries. Only 4 out of 45 countries received more than US$10 million annually (on average) over the period 2001–06 (see figure 3.9). The largest recipient was South Africa (US$17.4 million a year) followed by Ghana (US$17.1 million), Mozambique (US$16.9 million), and Ethiopia (US$11.3 million). No Francophone African countries received more than US$5 million a year over the period.

Another way to look at direct aid is to compare the total amount of aid to universities and research centers with the number of students enrolled in these institutions. As shown in figure 3.10, Mozambique received the

Figure 3.8 Total Aid to Africa for Higher Education, Commitments, 2002–06

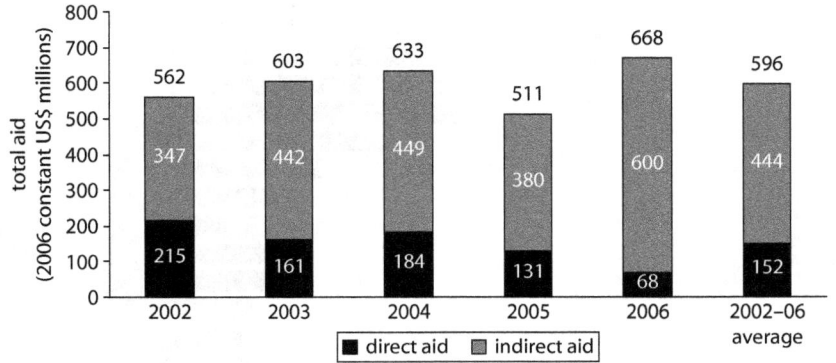

Source: OECD 2009.

Box 3.10

The Nature of Direct and Indirect Aid to Higher Education

Total amounts of aid to higher education hide very different types of assistance. Part of it goes directly to African universities and research centers (known as "direct aid to higher education"), while another significant portion of the total is made available to finance scholarships or to compensate institutions for the costs of African students in donors' countries (known as "indirect aid to higher education").

Assistance to higher education also derives from budget support. However, it is very difficult to assess the share of budget support allocated to higher education. Hence, these amounts are not included in the analysis.

Source: Authors.

---

highest amount of external aid per student enrolled in higher education (on average, US$595 per year between 2001 and 2006), followed by the Central African Republic (on average, US$427 per year between 2001 and 2006).

Part of direct aid to higher education supports universities and research centers in implementing their research and teaching programs. It can take the form of supply of equipment (IT, books), building of infrastructure, or financing of technical assistance to develop programs and curricula (see box 3.11). Several donors put a strong emphasis on language programs, aiming to foster the use of their language within partner universities. Finally, an analysis of donors' portfolios shows that

Figure 3.9 Direct Aid to Higher Education in Select African Countries, Annual Average Commitments, 2001–06

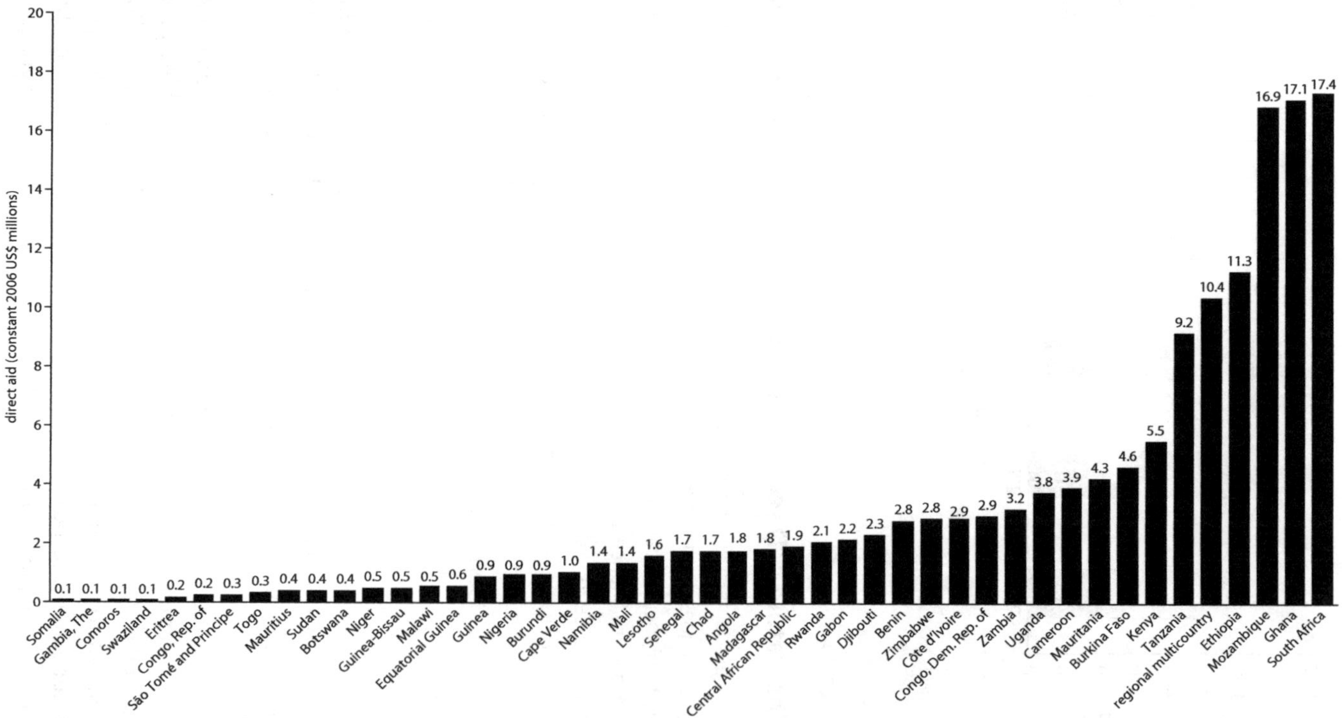

Country	direct aid (constant 2006 US$ millions)
South Africa	17.4
Ghana	17.1
Mozambique	16.9
Ethiopia	11.3
regional multicountry	10.4
Tanzania	9.2
Kenya	5.5
Burkina Faso	4.6
Mauritania	4.3
Cameroon	3.9
Uganda	3.8
Zambia	3.2
Congo, Dem. Rep. of	2.9
Côte d'Ivoire	2.9
Zimbabwe	2.8
Benin	2.8
Djibouti	2.3
Gabon	2.2
Rwanda	2.1
Central African Republic	1.9
Madagascar	1.8
Angola	1.8
Chad	1.7
Senegal	1.6
Lesotho	1.4
Mali	1.4
Namibia	1.4
Cape Verde	1.0
Burundi	0.9
Nigeria	0.9
Guinea	0.9
Malawi	0.6
Equatorial Guinea	0.5
Guinea-Bissau	0.5
Niger	0.5
Botswana	0.4
Sudan	0.4
Mauritius	0.4
Togo	0.3
São Tomé and Príncipe	0.2
Congo, Rep. of	0.2
Eritrea	0.1
Swaziland	0.1
Comoros	0.1
Gambia, The	0.1
Somalia	0.1

Source: OECD 2009.

Figure 3.10 Direct Aid to Higher Education per Student in Select African Countries, Annual Average Commitments, 2001–06

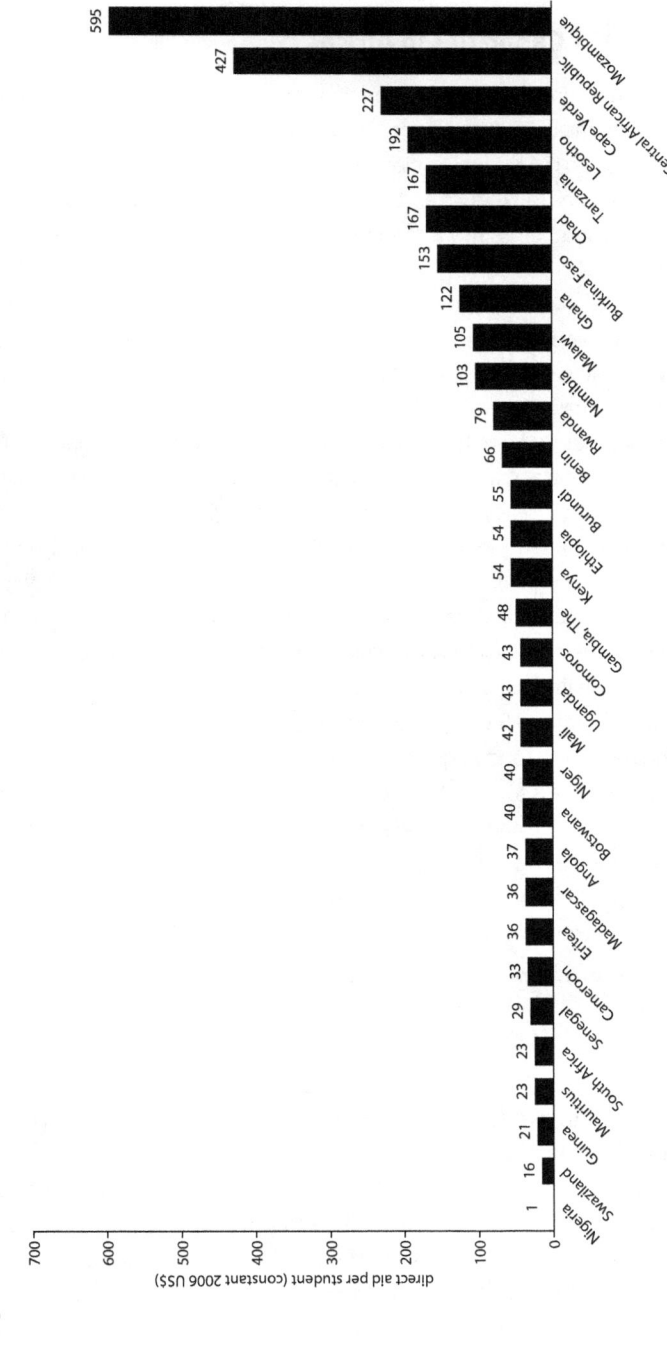

Source: OECD 2009.

Box 3.11

Building ICT Capacities in Africa

Recognizing the importance of information and communication technology (ICT) for development, in 2008, the European Commission allocated about US$600,000 over two years to the ICT for Development (ICT4D) Project. The ICT4D Project aims to build capacities to produce and use ICT for development purposes in eastern, western, and southern Africa through the sharing of expertise between existing networks in Africa and Europe. Participating universities include Edouardo Mondlane University (Mozambique), Maseno University (Kenya), Tumaini University (Tanzania), University of Education Winneba (Ghana), C. A. Diop University (Senegal), Royal Holloway and Bedford New College (United Kingdom), and University of Southern Denmark (Denmark).

Extensive networking through university staff and student exchanges, face-to-face workshops, and a virtual collaboration platform are expected to result in a cross-institutional research agenda and creation of regionally relevant curricula in ICT. The online platform serves as a means of communication and social networking for partners and staff. It includes discussion forums and archives for newly created ICT4D curriculum and learning materials. It is also a place for ICT4D instructors to search for the accumulated academic measures, syllabi, lesson plans, teaching activities, and learning materials created by other instructors. Intensive online collaboration between African and European partners also plays a crucial role in boosting networking and upgrading courses.

The project seeks to hone the theoretical and technical ICT skills of more than 2,000 undergraduate and postgraduate students and 200 researchers working in computer science or development. In the longer run, these figures will be much higher, and as the courses continue to be rolled out, the numbers participating in new courses developed as a result will accumulate.

Source: Consortium of African and European Higher Education Institutions 2008.

---

direct aid to higher education is highly fragmented and, as a result, has very limited impact in any given country. Over the period 2001–06, about 2,000 projects were reported to OECD by 28 bilateral or multilateral donors. Most of them (93 percent) amounted to less than US$1 million, and two-thirds of them (67 percent) amounted to less than US$100,000. In addition, most projects were carried out at the university or research center level. Only a handful of projects addressed the subsector in a holistic way and supported national strategies (see box 3.12).

Box 3.12

Support for Higher Education

Large projects supporting higher education as a whole are fairly rare. Over the period 2002 and 2006, only three countries received grants above US$15 million. In Mauritania, the Higher Education Project financed by the World Bank (US$15.8 million) was launched in 2004 and aimed to support the government's strategy for improving the skills of graduates. The project was designed to improve the quality of the learning environment and the relevance of courses to the labor market. Mozambique received US$76 million from the World Bank in 2002 to support higher education. Finally, Ethiopia received two significant grants between 2002 and 2006. In 2004, the World Bank allocated US$40 million for a project spanning 2004–08. This grant was supplemented by another US$18 million provided over seven years by the Netherlands for the Netherlands Government Program for Strengthening Post-Secondary Education and Training.

Sources: OECD 2009.

This situation is at odds with current trends in external assistance to education, in particular, primary education.

Indirect External Aid

In addition to direct support for higher education, most bilateral donors provide support to African students studying abroad. This support occasionally takes the form of scholarships, but most often the amount of aid is determined by imputing the cost of educating these students in foreign universities. Breaking down aid by types of support is difficult, as data are often fragmentary and not entirely reliable. On average, donors provided an estimated US$444 million annually to African students studying abroad during the period 2002–06. This is more than double the amount of direct aid to higher education, and this share rose significantly over the period.

Among African countries, students from Cameroon received in both absolute and relative terms the largest support for studying abroad (on average US$68 million annually) over 2001–06, followed by students from Senegal (US$46 million; see table 3.12). When compared to the number of international students, the amount of aid appears significant. Each student from Cameroon studying in a foreign university received more than US$5,000 a year during the period 2001–06, while this number was US$4,600 for Senegal and US$4,100 for Côte d'Ivoire.

Table 3.12 Indirect Aid to Higher Education in Select African Countries, Annual Average Commitments, 2001–06

Country	Scholarships and imputed student costs for students studying abroad (US$ millions)	Total number of students studying abroad	Aid per student studying abroad (US$)
Cameroon	68.1	12,651	5,382
Senegal	46.3	10,016	4,624
Côte d'Ivoire	21.6	5,236	4,117
Cape Verde	20.2	3,814	5,292
Madagascar	19.4	3,861	5,022
Congo, Rep. of	15.8	4,012	3,934
Gabon	15.7	3,365	4,671
Benin	13.6	2,836	4,805
Mauritius	12.3	6,330	1,946
Togo	10.5	2,665	3,931
Djibouti	10.4	1,820	5,734
Guinea	9.6	2,725	3,536
Mali	9.3	2,460	3,781
Ethiopia	8.3	3,033	2,732
Congo, Dem. Rep. of	8.0	2,927	2,740
Ghana	7.7	7,000	1,098
Sudan	7.5	2,700	2,774
Nigeria	6.7	14,739	457
Mauritania	6.6	1,837	3,589
Angola	6.2	5,819	1,071
Comoros	5.9	2,034	2,909
Burkina Faso	5.6	1,466	3,811
Rwanda	5.4	1,329	4,072
Kenya	5.4	12,860	420
Mozambique	5.3	2,369	2,223
Uganda	4.8	2,152	2,209
Tanzania	4.6	3,684	1,251
Central African Republic	3.7	1,032	3,610
Niger	3.6	1,131	3,216
Guinea-Bissau	3.1	601	5,220
South Africa	3.1	5,602	548
São Tomé and Principe	2.9	593	4,898
Chad	2.6	1,092	2,420
Burundi	2.0	606	3,266
Zambia	1.7	3,022	546
Sierra Leone	0.9	779	1,192
Zimbabwe	0.9	13,520	68
Equatorial Guinea	0.6	657	880
Eritrea	0.6	734	764

(continued)

Table 3.12 Indirect Aid to Higher Education in Select African Countries, Annual Average Commitments, 2001–06 *(continued)*

Country	Scholarships and imputed student costs for students studying abroad (US$ millions)	Total number of students studying abroad	Aid per student studying abroad (US$)
Somalia	0.3	954	298
Malawi	0.3	1,367	202
Namibia	0.3	5,694	46
Gambia, The	0.2	895	246
Seychelles	0.2	391	463
Botswana	0.2	7,670	20
Liberia	0.1	586	182
Lesotho	0.1	3,330	30
Swaziland	0.0	2,041	16

Source: OECD 2009.

Balance between Direct and Indirect Support

Support to higher education is biased toward indirect rather than direct support (see table 3.13). Only 4 out of the 31 countries for which data are available received more aid directly to their higher education system than through indirect support to students. The ratio is particularly high in countries such as Nigeria, Guinea, Cameroon, Senegal, and Madagascar. Although support to international students may assist African countries in their efforts to strengthen their own human resource base, international education can also result in a brain drain rather than the circulation of skills between host and home country. However, there are no systematic data on the relationship between the mobility of students and subsequent variation in patterns of immigration. Stay rates in countries following the completion of studies vary considerably depending on the country of origin and the academic discipline pursued (International Organization for Migration 2008). In most cases stay rates partly depend on the level of economic development of the country of origin (see box 3.13). This inevitably poses the question of whether indirect aid to higher education promotes growth and development.

Another effect of indirect aid is to drain African countries' own resources for higher education. One out of 16 African students studies abroad, in some cases with a scholarship from his or her own country. This is significantly higher than the global average of one out of 50 (UIS 2006). Europe and North America host about three-quarters of African

Table 3.13 Direct and Indirect Aid to Higher Education in Select African Countries, Annual Average Commitments, 2001–06

Country	Direct aid per student (A)	Indirect aid per international student (B)	Ratio A/B
Nigeria	1	457	688.0
Guinea	21	3,536	167.8
Cameroon	33	5,382	164.4
Senegal	29	4,624	158.4
Madagascar	36	5,022	138.0
Mali	42	3,781	89.5
Mauritius	23	1,946	85.6
Niger	40	3,216	79.8
Benin	66	4,805	72.5
Comoros	43	2,909	67.9
Burundi	55	3,266	59.8
Uganda	43	2,209	52.0
Rwanda	79	4,072	51.5
Ethiopia	54	2,732	50.8
Angola	37	1,071	29.2
Burkina Faso	153	3,811	25.0
South Africa	23	548	23.4
Cape Verde	227	5,292	23.3
Eritrea	36	764	21.0
Chad	167	2,420	14.5
Ghana	122	1,098	9.0
Central African Republic	427	3,610	8.4
Kenya	54	420	7.8
Tanzania	167	1,251	7.5
Gambia, The	48	246	5.1
Mozambique	595	2,223	3.7
Malawi	105	202	1.9
Swaziland	16	16	1.0
Botswana	40	20	0.5
Namibia	103	46	0.4
Lesotho	192	30	0.2

Source: OECD 2009.

foreign students. Given the high cost of studying in these countries, the total cost of the scholarships provided to these students represents a significant share of national budget for higher education. A sample of 19, mostly Francophone, African countries reveals that on average 18 percent of current public expenditure on higher education is spent supporting students abroad (table 3.7).

Box 3.13

How Many African Students Return to Their Country of Origin after Completing Their Studies?

Since such a high share of aid to higher education is used to finance African students in donors' universities, whether African students eventually return to Africa becomes a key issue. This is a difficult question to answer due to the lack of reliable and comprehensive data on the issue. In 2005, the Centre de Recherches sur l'Enseignement Supérieur (Center for Research on Higher Education) examined the case of foreign students in France. Ten universities were chosen along with a sample of 1,715 students, including 357 African students. The study shows that only 30 percent of African students in France wanted to return to their country of origin, compared with 45 percent of East Asian students. Although these figures have to be considered with caution due to their limited representativeness, the high stay rate of African students is certainly acute. More research needs to be done to assess the behavior of African students abroad and evaluate the impact of foreign indirect aid on economic and social development in Africa.

Source: Centre de Recherches sur l'Enseignement Supérieur 2007.

Foundation Support

In addition to bilateral donors, foundations have played a growing role in financing higher education in Africa. Since 2000, seven American foundations (namely, the Ford, Carnegie, Rockefeller, MacArthur, Hewlett, Mellon, and Kresge foundations) plus the Partnership for Higher Education in Africa have made significant investments in African universities. Between 2000 and 2008, the partnership foundations contributed an aggregate of US$354 million toward higher education initiatives in seven countries (Ghana, Kenya, Nigeria, Mozambique, South Africa, Tanzania, and Uganda) and on an Africa-wide basis (see figure 3.11).

The most significant focus of the partnership has been the development of universities' physical infrastructure and human and organizational capacity. Information technologies and connectivity to the Internet are at the core of these efforts, with investments to date of more than US$30 million. Outcomes from partners' investments range from more and cheaper Internet bandwidth for universities and the establishment of research and training networks in the sciences and social sciences to the launch of a new Internet gateway for the collection and dissemination of

Figure 3.11 Assistance from the Partnership for Higher Education in Africa, 2000–08

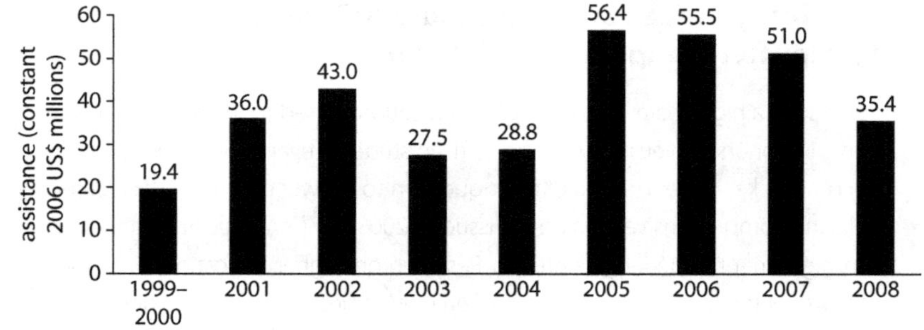

Year	Assistance (constant 2006 US$ millions)
1999–2000	19.4
2001	36.0
2002	43.0
2003	27.5
2004	28.8
2005	56.4
2006	55.5
2007	51.0
2008	35.4

Source: Partnership for Higher Education in Africa.

research. This includes more than US$7 million to establish the first regional satellite bandwidth consortium in Sub-Saharan Africa. The purchasing consortium not only provided the universities with more bandwidth at cheaper prices, but also influenced broader market pricing, encouraged universities to acquire hardware, and contributed to an increase in the use of ICT in teaching, learning, and research.

Examples of South-South cooperation are also growing. In 2001, the Aga Khan Foundation supported creation of the Advanced Nursing Studies Program in Kenya, Uganda, and Tanzania. The aim was to provide relevant, accessible, affordable, and needs-based training programs for nurses and midwives. The program builds on the knowledge, skills, and experience that nurses already possess. The program focuses on upgrading the skills of practicing nurses and providing graduate program opportunities for those seeking to further their nursing career at the leadership level. Furthermore, the program has been offered through a distance learning mode in Kenya since 2004. Distance learning opportunities were introduced in Tanzania and Uganda in 2006, which also allows students from Zanzibar to enroll in the program. As of 2008, 614 students were enrolled in the region, and there were 725 graduates of the Aga Khan University's Advanced Nursing Studies Program.[17]

External Aid for Research and Development

For decades, research development in Africa has been underpinned by aid, with the amounts varying greatly according to the country involved. The programs take diverse forms: fellowships for training, research grants to individuals and teams, institution building, strengthening and twinning arrangements, North-South partnership research programs, and so on (Gaillard 2000). Foreign funding agencies typically concentrate on particular institutions or faculties. For example, the Sokoine University of Agriculture in Tanzania is a typical case of external dependence (Sokoine University of Agriculture 2009).

To reduce dependency and strengthen a national approach to research development, the New Partnership for Africa's Development recommended measures and mechanisms to mobilize resources within a country through public and private sector investment in R&D and through research institutions.[18] In addition, it established S&T targets for government expenditure within its sector priorities (see table 3.14).

The Millennium Science Initiative, an international initiative designed to build capacity in modern science and engineering, is another example of international efforts to support efficient, nationally owned financing of R&D. Experience from developing countries has shown that focused investment in research excellence, awarded through competition and closely linked to training, can provide a catalytic stimulus for quality, relevance, and human capital development in S&T (World Bank 2008b).

The Millennium Science Initiative in Uganda, a five-year, US$33.35 million program started in 2006 with co-financing from the government of Uganda and the World Bank, is a central component of the government's strategy to strengthen the country's scientific and technological capacity (World Bank 2006b). It was planned in partnership with the Uganda National Council for Science and Technology, Uganda's Ministry of Finance, Planning, and Economic Development, and the World Bank.[19]

In addition, the Ugandan Parliament has endorsed a government policy to direct scholarships for study in public universities increasingly toward scientific and technology disciplines, with up to 70 percent of scholarships being earmarked for S&T and other areas of study deemed to be of critical economic importance.

Table 3.14 Targets for Expenditure on Select Sectoral Priorities

Sector	Percentage of allocation	Basis of allocation
Health	15	National budget
Agriculture	10	National budget, to be met within five years
Water and sanitation	5	Budgets at all levels of government (national and local)
Science and technology	1	GDP, to be met within five years

Source: United Nations, Secretary General 2004.

Mozambique, while acknowledging international funding partners, agencies, and instruments as a key source of funding for S&T, has also developed a series of national systems to promote S&T research. The Ministry of Science and Technology has elaborated a method for funding research by establishing an institutional grading system evaluated by the National Research Fund (see box 3.14).

External financing for higher education institutions in Africa remains scarce. Although external donors provide small amounts of aid directly to universities and research centers, the bulk of their assistance goes to

---

Box 3.14

The National Research Fund and Modalities of Funding in Mozambique

The National Research Fund is a national, independent institution, under the Ministry of Science and Technology, that invites proposals for funding, evaluates the proposals, awards funding, and monitors and evaluates the results of funded proposals as well as fund its own programs and projects that promote and enhance S&T in the country. The fund uses several funding instruments:

1. *Research projects.* Researchers are invited to submit research proposals for funding. These are adjudicated, and funding is awarded on a competitive basis, using published criteria.
2. *Institutional development.* For enhancement of Mozambique's research capacity, some funds are available to pay for additions to and improvements in the research infrastructure of research institutions. These funds are also made available on the basis of successful proposals.
3. *Government-commissioned research projects.* From time to time, the government identifies specific research projects that need urgent attention to address national priorities. This funding instrument is used to fund such projects.
4. *Innovation and technology transfer.* A portion of the fund's resources is used to fund the high-risk phases of the innovation and commercialization of new products and services as well as the transfer of technology. Funding is awarded on the basis of successful proposals.
5. *S&T development.* The fund is used to assist in creating a culture of S&T, to build awareness, to enhance S&T capabilities and capacities, and to support related initiatives. Both solicited and unsolicited proposals for funding are considered.

Source: Mozambique Council of Ministers 2006.

universities that host African students in their own country (see box 3.15). In parallel to official development assistance, the role of foundations has increased steadily since 2000, and they are now a major source of support for African universities. Going beyond the amount of aid, the modalities used do not seem to maximize impact, as specific and coordinated support for higher education still proves elusive. Much recent development activity at the higher education level has resulted from projects implemented by universities themselves, academic and university associations, and charitable foundations. Funding has been distributed among numerous agents aiming at different development processes, thus missing out on the potential to maximize impact through coordination. Donors need to revisit the way they support higher education systems in Africa if the impact is to be improved. The elaboration by African governments of national strategies for supporting higher education would certainly contribute to the emergence of coordinated and effective external support.

Box 3.15

Methodological Note

The analysis of official development assistance in this chapter is based on data from the OECD Creditor Reporter System On-line Database on Aid Activities. The system includes information from the Development Assistance Committee of the OECD countries, the European Commission, the World Bank, regional development banks, and some United Nations agencies. This discussion focuses on commitments for which the coverage is virtually complete. Using commitments implies some volatility in the data, since commitments are recorded for the year in which they are made, but are often disbursed over several years. To reduce the volatility of the data, an average over several years has generally been used throughout the chapter.

The Development Assistance Committee data enable the user to assess global amounts of aid to higher education and make international comparisons. However, the data are not entirely reliable, and donors do not always record their data accurately. In the field of higher education, donors may not record precisely the purpose of aid. Every effort has been made to disentangle the types of aid and direct, scholarship, or imputed student cost. While the big picture holds, disaggregated data may not be entirely accurate.

Notes

1. Because it has little or no logical basis, this process is sometimes called ad hoc budgeting.
2. A relatively rare approach employed by Togo and several Central American countries is to stipulate in the constitution that the education budget will be a fixed percentage of government spending. This tends to create financial instability, as institutional budgets fluctuate in accordance with the ups and downs of government revenues (Orr 2002).
3. In Kenya, the cost per student is not differentiated by disciplinary area and has remained unchanged since 1995 in spite of rising costs, thus rendering it obsolete (Ngome 2003).
4. Since the collapse of the former Soviet Union, which had developed and extensively used the method of normative unit costs, few countries have employed this approach (Adu and Orivel 2006).
5. For example, in 1995 Côte d'Ivoire created a Ministry of Higher Education and gave it responsibility for a collection of postsecondary educational institutions that had previously been housed within the ministries of agriculture, public works, finance, education, and professional technical training.
6. Any informed discussion of the strategic choices available to African countries regarding R&D requires a broader and more reliable availability of data. There are significant data gaps on the costs, financing (both budgetary and nonbudgetary), and research outputs at both the national and institutional levels for Sub-Saharan Africa.
7. The definitions given in this section draw heavily on Marcucci and Johnstone (2007).
8. The distinction between a tuition fee (and/or a registration fee) and other kinds of fees is imprecise but important, especially in Africa, where the term "fee" is sometimes deliberately used to hide what could just as well be termed tuition because of legal obstacles or political opposition to the very idea of such a fee. Tuition fees generally refer to mandatory charges levied upon all students (or their parents), which cover some portion of the general underlying instructional costs. A fee (other than tuition) generally refers to a charge levied to recover all or most of the expenses associated with a particular institutionally provided good or service such as student accommodation, which is frequently (though not always) used by some (but not all) students and might in other circumstances be privately provided. Other charges, which are less precisely distinct from a tuition fee because they are usually required of all students but are nonetheless based on the actual expense of the particular institutionally provided good or service, are levied to cover the cost of processing admission applications, administering examinations, or providing Internet access or recreational programs (Marcucci and Johnstone 2007).

9. Between 1973 and 1995, students in Botswana who benefited from the grant scheme were expected to contribute 5 percent of their initial gross salary for a stipulated period of time after graduating.
10. This increased from 55 to 76 percent in Côte d'Ivoire and from 19 to 30 percent in Guinea-Bissau.
11. Brossard and Foko (2008) point out important cross-country differences in expenditures on student welfare, ranging from less than 15 percent in Madagascar and Cameroon to more than 50 percent in Mali, Niger, and Senegal. A significant proportion of the spending on student welfare in Francophone Africa (average of 63 percent in the eight countries for which data are available: Benin, Côte d'Ivoire, the Republic of Congo, Guinea, Mauritania, the Central African Republic, Rwanda, and Senegal) is allocated to direct student transfers via food and housing, accommodation allowances, transportation allowances, and so forth.
12. The 2009 official exchange rate is used because the Ghanaian cedi was redenominated in 2007.
13. This is an approximation in view of the difficulty of collecting statistical information on private higher education.
14. A student loan program in Uganda is slated to start in the coming fiscal year. It will help privately sponsored students to cover tuition fees.
15. In Kenya, the Higher Education Loans Board (HELB) loans for module I students, private students, and module II students carry an interest rate of 4 percent. There is a lag of two years between the Kenya Certificate of Secondary Education (KCSE) and entrance at university for government-sponsored students. The students who took their KCSE in 2007, for example, enrolled in September 2009. Because of this, module II students also have to wait two years between the KCSE and their eligibility for an HELB loan.
16. "Deferment" refers to when loan repayments are postponed for some period of time due to additional study or economic hardship. No interest is accrued during the deferment period. "Forbearance" is similar, but while payments may be temporarily stopped in some cases (although interest continues to accrue), in other cases the individual repayment amounts are reduced or the repayment period is extended. A loan that combines features of a conventional fixed-schedule loan with income-contingent elements is sometimes referred to in the student loan literature as a "hybrid fixed-schedule, income-contingent loan plan."
17. http://www.partnershipsinaction.org/downloads/briefs/Advanced_Nurses_Studies_in_East_Africa.pdf.
18. First New Partnership for Africa's Development Ministerial Conference on Science and Technology, Johannesburg, South Africa, November 2003.
19. http://sites.ias.edu/sig/msi/initiatives.

References

Ade Ajayi, J. F., Lameck Goma, and G. Ampah Johnson. 1996. *The African Experience with Higher Education*. London: James Currey.

Adongo, Jonathan. 2008. *Higher Education in Namibia: Financing, Access, Equity, and Policy Reform*. Pretoria: Sizanang Centre for Research and Development/Ford Foundation.

Adu, Kingsley, and François Orivel. 2006. *Tertiary Education Funding Strategy in Ghana*. Accra: Ministry of Education, Sports, and Culture.

Aina, O. T. 2002. "Alternative Modes of Financing Higher Education in Nigeria and Implications for University Governance." *African Development* 27 (1): 236–62.

Brossard, Mathieu, and Borel Foko. 2008. *Costs and Financing of Higher Education in Francophone Africa*. Africa Human Development Series. Washington, DC: World Bank.

Centre de Recherches sur l'Enseignement Supérieur. 2007. *Observatoire de la vie étudiante*. Paris: Centre de Recherches sur l'Enseignement Supérieur.

Cheboi, Benjamin. 2008. *Student Loan Design*. Buffalo, NY: International Comparative Higher Education Finance and Accessibility Project.

Cheboi, Benjamin, and Roy Jackson. 2008. *Designing Systems for Student Loan Servicing and Collection*. Buffalo, NY: International Comparative Higher Education Finance and Accessibility Project.

Chilundo, Arlindo. 2008. "Access and Equity in Higher Education: Assessing Financing Policies in Mozambique." Unpublished manuscript. Department of Education, South Africa.

Consortium of African and European Higher Education Institutions. 2008. "Building ICT Capacities in Africa." ICT4D Project paper. http://www.acp-edulink.eu/Documents/EN-ICT4D.pdf.

Gaillard, Jacques. 2000. *Science in Africa at the Dawn of the 21st Century: Country Report; Tanzania*. Brussels: European Commission.

Girdwood, Alison. 1999. *Tertiary Education in Ghana: An Assessment 1988–1998*. Report 20261. Washington, DC: World Bank.

Hartnett, Teresa. 2000. "Financing Trends and Expenditure Patterns in Nigerian Federal Universities: An Update." World Bank, Washington, DC.

HESA (Higher Education South Africa). 2008. *Tuition Fees*. Pretoria: HESA.

International Association of Universities. 2007. *Guide to Higher Education in Africa*. 4th ed. New York: Palgrave MacMillan and the Association of African Universities.

International Comparative Higher Education Finance and Accessibility. 2008. *Database of Student Parent Cost by Country 2008*. http://www.gse.buffalo.edu/org/inthigheredfinance/index.html.

International Organization for Migration. 2008. *World Migration Report 2008: Managing Labour Mobility in the Evolving Global Economy.* Geneva: International Organization for Migration.

Jackson, Roy. 2002. "The National Student Financial Aid Scheme of South Africa (NAFAS): How and Why It Works." *Welsh Journal of Education* 11 (1): 82–94.

Johnstone, D. Bruce. 2003. "Cost Sharing in Higher Education: Tuition, Financial Assistance, and Accessibility." *Czech Sociological Review* 39 (3): 351–74.

———. 2004. "The Economics and Politics of Cost Sharing in Higher Education: Comparative Perspectives." *Economics of Education Review* 20 (4): 403–10.

———. 2006. "Higher Educational Accessibility and Financial Viability: The Role of Student Loans." In *Higher Education in the World 2006: The Financing of Universities,* ed. Joaquim Tres and Francisco L. Segrera. Barcelona: Palgrave Macmillan.

Jongbloed, Ben. 2000. "The Funding of Higher Education in Developing Countries." In *The Financing of Higher Education in Sub-Saharan Africa,* ed. Ben. Jongbloed and Hanneke Teekens. Utrecht: Cheps/Lemma.

Kharchi, Ahmed. 2003. "Mauritania." In *African Higher Education: An International Reference Handbook,* ed. Damtwe Teferra and Philip G. Altbach. Bloomington, IN: Indiana University Press.

Lewin, Keith M., Vuyelwa Ntoi, and N. H. J. Puleng Mapuru. 2000. "Costs and Financing of Teacher Education in Lesotho." Multi-Site Teacher Education Research Project. Centre for International Education, University of Sussex.

Manuh, Takyiwaa, Sulley Gariba, and Joseph Budu. 2007. *Change and Transformation in Ghana's Publicly Funded Universities.* Oxford: James Currey; Accra: Woeli Publishing Services.

Marcucci, Pamela N., and D. Bruce Johnstone. 2007. "Tuition Fee Policies in a Comparative Perspective: Theoretical and Political Rationales." *Journal of Higher Education Policy and Management* 29 (1): 25–40.

Materu, Peter. 2007. "Higher Education Quality Assurance in Sub-Saharan Africa: Challenges, Opportunities, and Promising Practices." African Human Development Series Working Paper 124, World Bank, Washington, DC.

Merisotis, Jamie. 2003. "Higher Education Funding in Ethiopia: An Assessment and Guidance for Next Steps." World Bank, Washington, DC.

Mozambique Council of Ministers. 2006. "MOSTIS (Mozambique Science, Technology, and Innovation Strategy) 2006." Report of the Council of Ministers in the 15th Regular Session. June.

Munene, Ishmael, and Wycliffe Otieno. 2008. "Changing the Course: Equity Effects and Institutional Risk amid Policy Shifts in Higher Education in Kenya." *Higher Education* 55 (4): 461–79.

Musisi, N. B. 2007. *Access and Equity in Higher Education: Assessing Financing Policies; A Comparative Study of African Countries—Uganda*. Pretoria: Sizanang Centre for Research and Development; Washington, DC: Ford Foundation.

Mwiria, Kilemi. 2003. "University Governance and University-State Relations." In *African Higher Education: An International Reference Handbook*, ed. Damtwe Teferra and Philip G. Altbach. Bloomington, IN: Indiana University Press.

Mwiria, Kilemi, Njuguna Ng'ethe, Charles Ngome, Douglas Ouma-Odero, Violet Wawire, and Daniel Wesonga. 2007. *Public and Private Universities in Kenya*. Oxford: James Currey; Nairobi: East African Educational Publishers.

National University of Lesotho. 2008. "Fee Structure for 2008/09 Academic Year." National University of Lesotho, Maseru.

Ngome, Charles. 2003. "Kenya." In *African Higher Education: An International Reference Handbook*, ed. Damtew Teferra and Philip G. Altbach. Bloomington, IN: Indiana University Press.

OECD (Organisation for Economic Co-operation and Development). 2009. "International Development Statistics: Online Databases on Aid and Other Resource Flows." OECD, Paris. http://www.oecd.org/dac/stats/idsonline.

Orr, Dominic. 2002. "An Inquiry into the Process of Allocating Funds from Government as the Major Stakeholder to Institutions of Higher Learning." University of Bath, International Centre for Higher Education Management.

———. 2005. "Can Performance-based Funding and Quality Assurance Solve the State vs. Market Conundrum?" *Higher Education Policy* 18 (1): 31–50.

Otieno, Wycliffe. 2008. *Access and Equity in Higher Education: Assessing Financing Policies in Kenya*. Washington, DC: Partnership for Higher Education in Africa.

Partnership for Higher Education in Africa.

Pillay, Pundy. 2004. "The South African Experience with Developing and Implementing a Funding Formula for the Tertiary Education System." *Journal of Higher Education in Africa* 2 (3): 19–36.

———. 2008. "Higher Education Funding Frameworks in SADC." In *Towards a Common Future: Higher Education in the SADC Region; Research Findings from Four SARUA Studies*, ed. Piyushi Kotecha. Johannesburg: Southern African Regional Universities Association.

———. 2009. "Challenges and Lessons from East and Southern Africa." In *Financing Access and Equity in Higher Education*, ed. Jane Knight. Rotterdam: Sense Publishing.

Pôle de Dakar. 2008. "Réformes de l'enseignement supérieur en Afrique: Eléments de cadrages." Pôle de Dakar, Bureau for Education in Africa, United Nations Educational, Scientific, and Cultural Organization, Dakar. http://www.poledakar.org.

Salmi, Jamil. 2008. *Financing and Governance of Tertiary Education in Madagascar.* Washington, DC: World Bank.

Salmi, Jamil, and Arthur M. Hauptman. 2006. "Innovations in Tertiary Education Financing: A Comparative Evaluation of Allocation Mechanisms." Education Working Paper 4, World Bank, Washington, DC.

SARUA (Southern African Regional Universities Association). 2009. *SARUA Handbook 2009: A Guide to the Public Universities of Southern Africa.* Johannesburg: SARUA.

Sayed, Yusuf, Ian MacKenzie, Adrienne Shall, and Joanna Ward. 2008. *Mainstreaming Higher Education in National and Regional Development in Southern Africa: A Regional Profile.* Johannesburg: Southern African Regional University Association.

Shen, Hua, and Adrian Ziderman. 2007. "Student Loans Repayment and Recovery: International Comparisons." IZA Discussion Paper 3588, Bonn, Institute for the Study of Labor.

Siphambe, H. K. 2008. *Access and Equity in Higher Education: Assessing Financing Policies; Botswana.* Pretoria: Sizanang Centre for Research and Development and the Ford Foundation.

Sokoine University of Agriculture. 2009. "University Fees and Other Financial Responsibilities for Undergraduates." Sokoine University of Agriculture, Morogoro. http://www.suanet.ac.tz/docs/fees2009.pdf.

Some, T. 2006. *Cost-sharing in Francophone West Africa: Student Resistance and Institutional Stability at the University of Ouagadougou, Burkina Faso.* Buffalo, NY: Department of Educational Leadership and Policy.

Sorlin, Sverker. 2007. "Funding Diversity: Performance-based Funding Regimes as Drivers of Differentiation in Higher Education Systems." *Higher Education Policy* 20 (4): 413–40.

Steen, Edward. 2008. "Bringing Africa up to Speed on Science." *EuropeanVoice.com*, February 28.

Taskforce for the Development of the National Strategy for University Education. 2008. *Investing in the Future of University Education: The National Strategy for University Education, 2007–2015.* Nairobi: Ministry of Higher Education, Science, and Technology.

Thompson, Q. 2001. *Uganda Higher Education Strategy: Management and Financing of Higher Education.* Washington, DC: World Bank.

UIS (UNESCO [United Nations Educational, Scientific, and Cultural Organization] Institute for Statistics). 2006. *Global Education Digest 2006.* Montreal: UNESCO.

United Nations, Secretary General. 2004. *NEPAD: Second Consolidated Report on Progress in Implementation and International Support.* New York: United Nations.

University of Botswana. 2009. "Schedule of Fees 2009–2010." University of Botswana, Gaborone. http://www.ub.bw/documents/StudentFees2009-10 Circulate.pdf.

University of Dar es Salaam. 2009. "Revised Tuition Fees 2009/2010 Academic Year." University of Dar es Salaam, Dar es Salaam. http://www.udsm.ac.tz/userfiles/file/Undergraduate_fees_2009_2010.pdf.

University of Zambia. 2008. "Tuition Fees, Other Fees, and Accommodation Charges for Zambia Students: 2008 Academic Year." University of Zambia, Lusaka. http://www.unza.zm/index.php?option=com_content&task=view&id=50&Itemid=64.

University World News. 2009. "Francophone African: Under-funded, Overcrowded." February 8.

Varghese, N. V. 2004. *Private Higher Education in Africa.* Paris: International Institute for Educational Planning, United Nations Educational, Scientific, and Cultural Organization.

Woodhall, Maureen. 1991. *Student Loans in Higher Education: English-Speaking Africa.* Educational Forum Series 3. Paris: International Institute for Educational Planning.

World Bank. 2005. *Education Statistics.* Washington, DC: World Bank. http://go.worldbank.org/ITABCOGIV1.

———. 2006a. "Nigeria, Science and Technology Education at Post-basic Level (STEPB): Review of S&T Education in Federally Funded Institutions." Africa Region Human Development Department, World Bank, Washington, DC.

———. 2006b. "Project Information Document for Millennium Science Initiative, Uganda." World Bank, Washington, DC.

———. 2007a. "Cultivating Knowledge and Skills to Grow African Agriculture." Agriculture and Rural Development Department, World Bank, Washington, DC.

———. 2007b. *Le système éducatif tchadien: Elements de diagnostic pour une politique éducative nouvelle et une meilleure efficacité de la dépense publique.* Washington, DC: World Bank.

———. 2008a. *Accelerating Catch-up: Tertiary Education for Growth in Sub-Saharan Africa.* World Bank, Washington, DC.

———. 2008b. "Project Appraisal Document: Science and Technology Higher Education Program, Tanzania." World Bank, Washington, DC.

———. 2008c. *Le système éducatif beninois: Analyse sectorielle pour une polique educative plus équilibrée et plus efficace.* Washington, DC: World Bank.

———. 2009a. "Country Strategy Report: Rwanda 2009." World Bank, Washington, DC.

———. 2009b. *World Development Indicators*. Washington, DC: World Bank.

Ziderman, Adrian. 2004. *Policy Options for Student Loan Schemes: Lessons from Five Asian Case Studies*. Bangkok: International Institute for Educational Planning; Paris: United Nations Educational, Scientific, and Cultural Organization.

Ziderman, Adrian, and Douglas Albrecht. 1995. *Financing Universities in Developing Countries*. Washington, DC: Falmer Press.

CHAPTER 4

Tools for Financially Sustainable Tertiary Education Policies

Some African countries have implemented innovative and brave measures to deal with the rapid increase in the number of students, which, in view of limited resources, gives grounds for concern over the quality of educational programs. If these measures are coordinated and adapted to national conditions, they may guide government policies in identifying viable solutions to the challenges posed by higher education financing. The measures in question include (a) optimal mobilization and improved use of public resources, which in many countries still constitute the main source of financing; (b) reorientation of student flows over the entire education system and within higher education to better manage the number of students and ensure that the education received matches the needs of the labor market of the local economies; (c) diversification of financing sources, particularly by sharing the costs of education with the beneficiaries; (d) promotion of the private sector; (e) development of income-generating activities by higher education institutions; and (f) the organization of distance education programs.

Improving the Management of Public Financing

Increased public allocations to higher education can result from either an improvement in public finances or budget trade-offs in favor of the education sector (or both). Regarding improvements in public finance, there is a risk that the global financial crisis may undermine economic development in many countries, making them unable to add to the tax load without aggravating their population's conditions. Regarding the possibility of budget trade-offs, the situation varies from country to country. The share of recurrent expenditure allocated to education ranges from 3.0 percent (Equatorial Guinea) to 34.6 percent (Uganda), with a 46-country average of 17.7 percent. Similarly, education spending as a share of gross domestic product (GDP) ranges from 8 percent (the Democratic Republic of Congo) to 40 percent (Nigeria), with a 46-country average of 20.9 percent. Raising the level of resources allocated to the education sector as a whole seems difficult for countries in the upper part of that range, such as Kenya, Zimbabwe, Burundi, and Lesotho, but more feasible for countries in the lower part, such as Mali, Chad, Zambia, Guinea, and the Democratic Republic of Congo. Education, however, competes with other priority sectors such as health, security, and agriculture. Accordingly, any increase in public resources channeled to education will depend on the quality of the sector's strategy and plan as well as on the performance of the relevant minister or ministers in determining the trade-offs during budgetary negotiations.

Moreover, the level of higher education financing depends on trade-offs within the education budget itself. Here also, the situation varies considerably among African countries. The share of higher education in the education budget ranges from 4.1 percent (Cape Verde) to 39.1 percent (Lesotho), with a 39-country average of 21.2 percent. An increase in the share allotted to higher education is more justifiable in the case of countries close to achieving universal primary school enrollment. However, many countries (Namibia, for instance) are still far from attaining the Millennium Development Goal of Education for All and would therefore find it difficult to raise higher education's share of its education budget.

Nonetheless, the possibility of mobilizing additional resources for the sector should not be discounted. Experience shows that the higher education subsector will be able to mobilize public financing, especially internationally, for specific projects provided it can demonstrate that a given investment will yield social benefits and contribute to the more efficient use of resources.

Improving Budget Management

It is increasingly clear that African governments ought to be considering the adoption of performance-based budget allocations in place of historically determined allocations. Doing so would create a mechanism for correcting major institutional imbalances that have developed through the years. It would also inject greater transparency into the process, which would respond in part to growing demands for accountability in the use of public and private financing. In addition, performance-based allocations would advance the cause of institutional autonomy as institutions must function under full management control if they are to be judged on the basis of their performance. Moreover, it would facilitate revisions in the cost structure for higher education in those countries where *licence-master-doctorat* (LMD) reforms are being implemented in line with the Bologna process.

As outlined in chapter 3, African governments have used various methods to carry out budgetary planning for higher education. Among these, the most prominent have been historically based budgets, earmarked funding, formula funding, performance contracts, and competitive funding.[1] All of these provide resources directly to tertiary institutions from the Ministry of Finance, which may delegate some of its funds and authority for doing so to the Ministry of Education or to a higher education oversight body. The advantages and disadvantages associated with direct funding mechanisms are presented in table 4.1.

Historically Based Budgets

Historical or ad hoc budgeting is attractive because it is less time-consuming, requires no special technical skills or databases, and offers the implicit incentive of possibly getting more for an institution than it might otherwise deserve. Its disadvantages are that it is not strategic, it rewards good and bad institutional performance equally, it contains inherent motivation to expand enrollment in "cheaper" disciplines rather than more expensive ones (some of which may provide human resources essential for the country's future development), and it strongly reinforces the status quo in which the most established institutions tend to be the primary beneficiaries. Historical budgets also tend to favor expenditures linked with obvious advocates (for example, staff, students) over those with no advocates (for example, maintenance of buildings and grounds). A further concern is that in the minority of universities that choose their rectors or vice chancellors on the basis of internal voting by staff and students, the university community's choice of leadership may

Table 4.1 Advantages and Disadvantages of Various Funding Mechanisms

Type of mechanism	Advantages	Disadvantages
Historical budgeting	Has simplicity; has necessary capacities and procedures in place; contains cost growth	Maintains the status quo; is opaque, not strategic, not objective, and largely inflexible; does not improve access; does not improve performance; may distort enrollment profiles
Earmarked funding	Is tightly targeted; responds quickly; is transparent; can improve quality and relevance; can correct imbalances and inequities	Does not improve access; is problem specific; is not related to performance; period of use is unpredictable; is vulnerable to charges of "favoritism"
Formula funding	Is transparent; respects institutional autonomy; steers toward policy goals; can improve internal efficiency; is predictable	Requires new procedures and new capacities; is dependent on data quality; is comparatively labor intensive
Performance contract	Has strong alignment with strategic vision; has fewer labor requirements for financial management; can improve internal efficiency	Has difficult and ultimately subjective monitoring; tends to be punitive in orientation
Competitive funding	Respects institutional autonomy; can encourage junior staff; stimulates innovation; can improve external efficiency; is flexible in adjusting to new needs	Is not useful for systemwide reform; does not work well where large differences in institutional capacity exist; can be labor intensive

Sources: Salmi and Hauptman 2006; Saint 2006.

be influenced by perceptions of the candidate's ability to expand the institution's budget through political ties and access to decision makers.

Earmarked Funding

Funding set-asides are useful instruments for addressing ingrained resource allocation imbalances within a higher education system and for publicly signaling government's commitment to corrective action. South Africa has made good use of this mechanism in rectifying resource inequities among institutions that characterized the apartheid regime. However, earmarked funding is best used for finite periods to avoid becoming the source of new imbalances or losing political support for explicit "favoritism." In general, experience suggests that earmarked funds are better suited for financing capital investment projects rather than operational expenditures (Salmi and Hauptman 2006). In some cases, earmarked funds have been linked with specific sources of government revenue such as the Ghana Education Trust Fund (see box 4.1) or the Programme d'Urgence pour les Universités (Emergency Program for Universities) in Côte d'Ivoire, which has been financed by revenues received from the sale of public enterprises (see box 4.2).

Formula Funding

As noted, formula funding can range from the relatively simple (for example, staff head counts or student enrollment) to the exceedingly complex (for example, normative cost calculations by discipline and level of study). As the complexity increases, so do demands within the budgeting process for standardized data collection, organizational capacity, associated staff training, and professionally qualified management.

Box 4.1

Ghana Education Trust Fund

In 2000, the Ghanaian Parliament established the Ghana Education Trust (GET) Fund as a means of financing a more rapid expansion of the country's education system than was possible on the basis of the government budget alone. The fund was capitalized by increasing the existing value added tax by 2.5 percent. These revenues are earmarked for capital projects in the education sector, and their use for recurrent expenditures such as salaries is prohibited. By 2007, the GET Fund was generating roughly US$200 million annually. Tertiary education has received approximately 45 percent of GET funds since its inception. Its beneficiaries are the staff and students of Ghana's universities, polytechnics, and technical training institutes. GET funding has been used to construct educational facilities, capitalize a student loan program, provide scholarships for poor students and staff development, expand information and communication technology (ICT) infrastructure, and support research and teaching activities, particularly the expansion of postgraduate programs and distance education. The fund is governed by an independent board of trustees accountable to Parliament and managed by a government-appointed administrator. Each year the fund's allocation and its specific uses are approved by Parliament to ensure that they address the nation's most pressing education needs.

Sources: Atuahene 2008; Adu and Orivel 2006.

> **Box 4.2**
>
> **Emergency Universities Program in Côte d'Ivoire**
>
> Between 1993 and 2000, the government of Côte d'Ivoire put in place a significant investment program for the development of public universities. Coordinated by the Ministry of Higher Education, it was financed from revenues generated by the sale of public enterprises (for example, electricity, water supply, automotive regulation) to private investors. The program was implemented over the medium term on the basis of receipts totaling roughly US$100 million. It has enabled the improvement and expansion of existing university facilities as well as the construction of four new decentralized university campuses within the country.
>
> *Source:* Gioan 2007.

For example, performance-based formulas differ from most other allocation approaches in that they tend to use performance indicators that reflect public policy objectives rather than institutional needs, for example, graduate output or research productivity. The development of appropriate indicators and methodologies for tracking them is a challenging process of balancing what is ideal with what is feasible and of deciding when the ideal is sufficiently important that a significant investment in monitoring capacities and system development is warranted. Many countries use some type of funding formula based on actual costs per student. Bulgaria, the Czech Republic, United Kingdom, Ghana, and Nigeria use formulas based on normative student costs, while Denmark, United Kingdom, Israel, and the Netherlands use performance-based funding formulas.

Formula-based budgeting has several advantages. First, its greater transparency in budgetary allocations through the use of a publicly announced standard methodology helps to shield the process from political influence and enables institutional managers to predict the likely outcomes for planning purposes (Salmi and Hauptman 2006). Second, its capacity to provide resources commensurate with the true costs of an educational activity reduces internal cross-subsidies from more efficient programs to less efficient ones and helps to eliminate undesirable incentives to increase enrollment in low-cost disciplines. Third, funding formulas allow governments to avoid the use of potentially contentious policy directives that may be seen to interfere with university autonomy (Orr 2005). Instead, the formula simply makes them financially attractive to the institutions. Finally, its potential for steering the entire system in the direction of key policy goals through the inclusion of incentives for institutional improvement is its biggest innovation over previous budgeting methods. This characteristic enables funding formulas to be employed as powerful mechanisms for institutional change and system reform.

However, a funding formula can only be employed when institutions have the autonomy necessary to control the parameters of their main expenditures, for example, enrollment, staff salaries, and student fees. In many African, particularly Francophone, countries, this is not possible under the current regulatory frameworks for higher education. For example, where academic staff are considered to be public servants, decisions on the hiring, firing, and salaries of staff will be made by the public service commission or the ministry of finance rather than by the university. Other operational requirements for formula funding include standardized data gathering that enables comparable institutional statistics, agreement by ministry of finance officials to accept this new way of budgeting, and a strategic vision for the sector that offers guidance in shaping the funding formula.

As suggested, the disadvantages of formula funding are linked to its higher requirements for standardized data-gathering systems that generate comparable statistics in a timely manner for use in budgeting. In a multi-institutional higher education system, this effort must often begin by reaching agreement among the institutions' finance officers (and their superiors) on standard definitions for each accounting code that will be employed by all, including the important determination of whether a particular expense is classified as development or recurrent. Failure to achieve consistency in the classification of expenditures can distort the formula outcomes and undermine the credibility of the budgeting process. Appreciation of this fact, for example, led the National Universities Commission in Nigeria to undertake an extensive series of discussions with its two dozen federal universities earlier this decade aimed at developing a uniform accounting code for the entire university system. A common manual for this purpose was ultimately produced, but remains unused for reasons that are not clear.

Performance Contracts
Performance contracts are essentially tools for negotiated institutional change.[2] Government policy makers are willing to pay for the changes they view as needed, and university leaders realize that lack of cooperation

may lead to institutional penalties. As a result, the issue of how much change for how much money becomes the essence of the negotiations. In this process, all institutions may not have to live with equal outcomes, and systemic reform becomes the aggregate of individual institutional changes. Much depends on the energy and commitment of government leaders during the negotiation process and the political backing they receive. But where dynamic and sustained leadership exists, significant reform can be achieved in a relatively short period of time. However, changes in leadership in the ministry or oversight body charged with managing the performance contracts raise the risk of discontinuity or change of direction. Here, too, the use of appropriately chosen and verifiable indicators of performance is a condition for the effective use of this method. Internationally, performance contracts have been used by Austria, Denmark, Finland, France, Spain, and Switzerland.

Even more than in the case of formula funding, success with performance contracts seems to require strong leadership. Personal judgment and leadership style on the part of the government make a difference in deciding whether or not to hold an institution accountable for the fulfillment of its contract or whether intervening variables may justify a degree of compromise. Similar qualities are required for institutional leaders to ensure that the negotiated performance targets are realistic and not excessively disruptive to the daily operation of the institution. Leadership shortcomings on either side can easily provoke dissatisfaction within government or backlash from university staff and students. Recent university protests in France bear witness to this risk.

Competitive Funds
Competitive funding mechanisms have come into widespread use throughout the world, although their adoption in Africa has been much slower. This approach to funding is a cost-efficient way of stimulating desirable changes because the funds awarded come in addition to the institution's regular operating budget, providing a tangible incentive to participate in the competition. Yet the amount of funding necessary to operate a competitive fund is relatively small, often no more than 5 percent of the system's entire recurrent budget. Competitive funding also offers the advantage of respecting university autonomy by allowing staff to choose whether or not to participate and, if they do, by giving them a fair degree of freedom in defining the content of their funding proposals within the general guidelines of the competition. An important side benefit is institutional capacity building in the design and management of

projects. For junior staff, it may provide a first experience in preparing a funding proposal. For departments, it may create an opportunity for staff to collaborate around common interests and begin to develop a degree of comparative expertise. For university administrative services, it may help to develop financial management and procurement skills. Professional networking is another potential benefit, as recipients with similar interests are provided with opportunities to review each other's work and share results. Competitive funds for higher education have been employed by some 30 developing and developed countries including Argentina, Chile, Ghana, Indonesia, Jordan, the Russian Federation, South Africa, Tunisia, and the United States (Saint 2006).

Competitive funding also has disadvantages. In some cases, such as Ethiopia's World Bank–financed Post-Secondary Education Project, the capacity of universities to develop competitive funding proposals proved greater than the ministry's capacity to process funding agreements, monitor progress, and disburse funding on schedule. In many cases, weaker institutions display similar weaknesses in project management and financial administration. It is therefore important to recognize that fund management is labor intensive, demands high levels of organizational skill, and requires competency in procurement. These shortcomings argue for the importance of thorough capacity assessment together with targeted training as part of the design process for competitive funds. Financial sustainability for these funds once the donor withdraws has also been a challenge. Within Africa, only Ghana seems to be registering some progress in persuading the government to take on this commitment. On balance, competitive funds have proved more effective at encouraging discrete improvements (and occasional innovations) in teaching, program quality, and management effectiveness than in provoking institutional reforms or systemic changes (Saint 2006; see box 4.3).

African and international experience with competitive funds points to the need to consider three operational issues when designing a new fund (Salmi and Hauptman 2006). The first is how to create a common environment and fair access in diversified systems that contain both strong and weak tertiary education institutions. This is commonly tackled by creating separate categories in which similarly endowed institutions compete among themselves. In Ghana, for example, universities and polytechnics each contend within their respective categories. Likewise, in Mozambique the nation's three oldest public tertiary institutions were precluded from competing with newer and smaller institutions. A second issue is whether private institutions should be allowed to take part.

> **Box 4.3**
>
> **Mozambique's Competitive Fund for Tertiary Education**
>
> Mozambique's higher education system expanded rapidly over the past decade. In the process, student access has been disproportionately concentrated in the capital city, and perceptions of declining educational quality have become widespread. To address these problems, a competitive fund for higher education, called the Quality Enhancement and Innovation Fund (QIF), was set up in 2002. QIF operates on the basis of competitive application and merit-based evaluation by a permanent committee assisted by subject area specialists, using publicly announced criteria and procedures. The competition was open to public and private institutions for development initiatives (maximum of US$250,000) and to individuals for teaching innovation and research (maximum of US$25,000). Development awards to private institutions were treated as loans; all other awards were grants.
>
> Six years later, QIF has disbursed US$3.8 million to Mozambique's higher education system. A total of 51 projects have been approved out of 154 submissions. Private institutions received 30 percent of these awards. Institutional development funding has been used largely to acquire computers and related communication technologies, purchase Internet access, and apply these technologies to teaching and research. Innovation grants generally have focused on improving teaching practices in part through experimentation with new course designs. Research grants have enabled course content to be updated on the basis of local information, while exposing numerous students to a research experience.
>
> A recent impact evaluation noted that through its development grants, QIF has expanded higher education outside of the capital city. Additionally, it has helped to shore up educational quality through investments in teaching infrastructure, experimental teaching programs, training, and national networking. QIF also has provided many junior staff with experience in competitive funding and proposal preparation. Moreover, it has served as an instructive example to other government agencies operating beyond the scope of education.
>
> *Source:* Brouwer and others 2008.

Prevailing wisdom suggests that they should because they form part of the tertiary system, can occasionally be important sources of innovation, and contribute to a more stimulating, competitive environment. In practice, however, this is not always the case. Ethiopia precluded private universities from participating in its competitive fund. Ghana allowed participation, but regulated it rather tightly. Mozambique permitted full and nearly equal participation. A third question is whether access to the competitive fund should be linked to accreditation or similar quality assurance requirements to ensure that public funds strengthen programs that have already achieved a minimum level of excellence. The answer to this question is less clear, although it does provide an incentive for universities to seek accreditation. But what is clear is the need for accreditation criteria to be value neutral with regard to promoting any particular model of higher education provision (for example, the traditional residential multidisciplinary university). If they are not, then accreditation may well encourage uniformity instead of diversity and thus impede institutional innovation (see box 4.4; Ng'ethe, Subotzky, and Afeti 2008).

Box 4.4

International Experience with Competitive Funds

Well-designed competitive funds can stimulate the performance of tertiary education institutions and serve as powerful vehicles for their transformation and innovation. Argentina's Quality Improvement Fund has encouraged universities to engage in strategic planning to strengthen existing programs and create new interdisciplinary graduate programs. Within universities, faculties that had never worked together started cooperating in the design and implementation of joint projects. In Indonesia, World Bank projects that began in 1993 have stimulated ownership of new paradigms in tertiary education by the entire academic community. In the Arab Republic of Egypt, the Engineering Education Fund was instrumental in introducing the notion of competitive bidding and peer evaluation in the allocation of public investment resources. The fund helped to transform traditional engineering degrees into more applied programs with close linkages to industry. A competitive fund in Jordan follows detailed guidelines that are described in an operations manual and relies on international peer reviewers to evaluate projects of national interest. In Chile, a second wave of tertiary education reforms is being supported by a competitive fund for diversification (development of the nonuniversity sector, including private technical institutes) and quality improvement among all tertiary education institutions. Competitive funds have also been financed directly by governments. Examples can be found in Tanzania (Commission for Science and Technology), South Africa (Technology and Human Resources for Industry Programme), and the United States (Fund for the Improvement of Post-Secondary Education).

Sources: World Bank 2002; Saint 2006.

More Efficient Use of Available Resources

A reliable and effective information, evaluation, and monitoring system is a prerequisite for improving the use of public resources. Political decision makers and managers of higher education systems must have an overview of the use of allocations and monitor the effectiveness with regard to the achievement of objectives and transparency of procurement. The administration must therefore build dependable information systems, appropriate indicators, and benchmarks. Regular control and evaluation mechanisms must be set up. Consequently, the staff of monitoring teams within the ministries and the higher education institutions must be appropriately trained and conversant with the use of such tools, which must be part of their work culture. Budget and operational audits may result in the creation or consolidation of a database enabling managers to assess the efficiency of public expenditure. Confronted in the late 1990s with a severe financing crisis in a context of limited public resources, Côte d'Ivoire successfully implemented such procedures (see box 4.5).

Since salaries are the largest item of current expenditure, improving the management and redeployment of personnel can help to control

---

Box 4.5

A Plan for Streamlining Higher Education in Côte d'Ivoire

To deal with a swift increase in the number of higher education students (when elimination of the first stage of the *baccalauréat*, the school-leaving exam, nearly doubled the number of high school graduates), Ivorian political leaders implemented a plan in the late 1990s for streamlining the management of public higher education institutions. The plan was designed to ensure better use of public resources. Building on the results of budgetary and operational audits, it allowed a significant reduction in education unit costs in areas where they had been prohibitive, such as the *grandes écoles* in Yamoussoukro. The plan was implemented during a period of four years without a decline in the quality of training, and the average unit costs in those institutions decreased from CFAF 4.8 million to CFAF 2.1 million per student per year. Similarly, with regard to the training of secondary education teachers, unit costs decreased from CFAF 13 million to CFAF 5 million over a four-year period, mainly through the recruitment of future teachers at *licence* (bachelor's degree) rather than *baccalauréat* level.

Source: Gioan 1995.

expenditure. Extensive imbalances in the distribution of personnel are common. In some cases, student-teacher ratios of more than 100 students to one instructor in general education areas occur alongside rates of four or five students to one instructor in more specialized or technological disciplines, when an average rate of 10 or 12 students to one instructor would be more in line with accepted standards. Reducing such disparities requires the introduction of procedures for recruiting and posting lecturers according to a plan based on teaching staff standards and statutory annual workloads. A more systematic use of temporary lecturers would further help to curb the wage bill, especially where the employment of a full-time instructor is not justified or highly specialized instruction is required. Finally, establishing a specific status for technological and vocational instructors, who, contrary to university professors, do not necessarily have research obligations in addition to teaching, would allow for heavier teaching loads, thereby reducing the operational costs of technological and vocational programs. Tunisia, for instance, has created for its higher institutes of technological studies a corps of technology instructors expected to teach more hours than university professors. A similar status exists in Mauritania. With regard to administrative and technical personnel, more systematic recourse to subcontracting for some activities (including open space maintenance, cleaning, maintenance, and catering) could help to eliminate frequently observed redundancies.

Expenditure may be further streamlined by restructuring the supply of education and by improving the procedures for managing and monitoring expenditures. Restructuring the education supply in the framework, for instance, of the LMD reform undertaken in various French-speaking African countries, may involve the gradual elimination of disciplines not particularly relevant to a country's development. It could also lead to economies of scale if only by grouping together training programs that overlap or are attended by a small number of students. There are various possible ways to refocus the available resources to make them more effective. Reducing unit costs also requires greater rigor and transparency in the management of expenditures. Implementing financial audits often reveals procedural irregularities with regard to, among others, tendering and delivery control. Those are further opportunities for reducing unit costs and enhancing public expenditure efficiency.

Managing the Trends in Student Flows

The state and the educational institutions should ensure that students are oriented according to the needs of the labor market. This requirement is both economic (seeking a better match between education and both the human resource needs of the economic sectors and the reduction of unemployment among young graduates) and social (seeking a higher return on private investment in skills acquisition). Providing guidance throughout the school career implies selectivity of education programs. This raises political and technical issues. First, decision makers must identify ways of ensuring that the selection is socially fair, based on academic merit, and clearly aimed at meeting specific needs in qualified personnel. Second, they must avail themselves of economic forecasting tools and cooperate with the professionals of the sectors concerned to assess short- and medium-term requirements. Moreover, they should provide mechanisms for offering students and families information on the programs available at all levels of the education system, particularly in higher education, and on the respective employment prospects. Guidance, therefore, must seek to match labor market needs with the students' occupational plans and scholastic and personal aptitudes. This chapter deals solely with the quantitative aspects of flow management and student admission upstream from and at the entrance to higher education and at other levels of education.

The economies of African countries, which are still largely undiversified and informal, cannot absorb the increasing number of higher education graduates in disciplines not always relevant to local development. Yet Africa's strong demographic pressure and progress in primary school enrollment automatically increase the number of candidates seeking to enter secondary and higher education.[3] In many countries, the linear organization of schooling encourages students to prolong their studies as much as possible. This often leads to higher rates of unemployment, underemployment, or emigration of degree holders whose training does not correspond to their country's economic realities. Thus, for instance, although the human resources needed by African economies are mainly at the intermediate level and in agriculture (a sector often disregarded by the universities), only 8 percent of secondary education students in 2004/05 were registered in technical and vocational areas.[4] A systemic approach is therefore necessary to organize a viable—namely, more realistic and relevant—system of education. Upstream from higher education, flow management should consist of proposing at the end of primary education, technical lower secondary education, and upper technical secondary education alternatives clearly designed to accelerate integration into the labor market. Those alternatives should be coupled with reorientation courses for upgrading skills on a lifelong basis.

Better flow management in secondary education could have considerable impact on the future number of higher education students. According to simulations carried out in Mali in 2005 (see figure 4.1), if the annual increase in the number of students obtaining the *baccalauréat* were limited to 4 percent compared to the 11 percent trend rate, the number of higher education students in 2015 would be an estimated 95,000 compared to 160,000, respectively (Gioan 2005). Such a step should be considered in seeking an optimal compromise among change in the number of students, the amount of resources that may be mobilized, and the quality of education delivered.

Some countries have opted for selective admission into higher education. In some English-speaking countries (see, for instance, Kenya; see Otieno 2008), access to higher education is not automatic for secondary education graduates. In other countries, the state covers education costs for only some higher education candidates (see the case of Uganda; Musisi and Mayega 2007), while the remaining prospective students must finance their own studies possibly with the help of public or private loans when such credit is available. In French-speaking countries, however, such selection is not as easy to implement, mainly because the *baccalauréat* is viewed as providing automatic access to higher education (see box 4.6).

Figure 4.1 Estimated Number of Higher Education Students in Mali, Assuming Current Trends and Regulations in Secondary Education, 2005–16

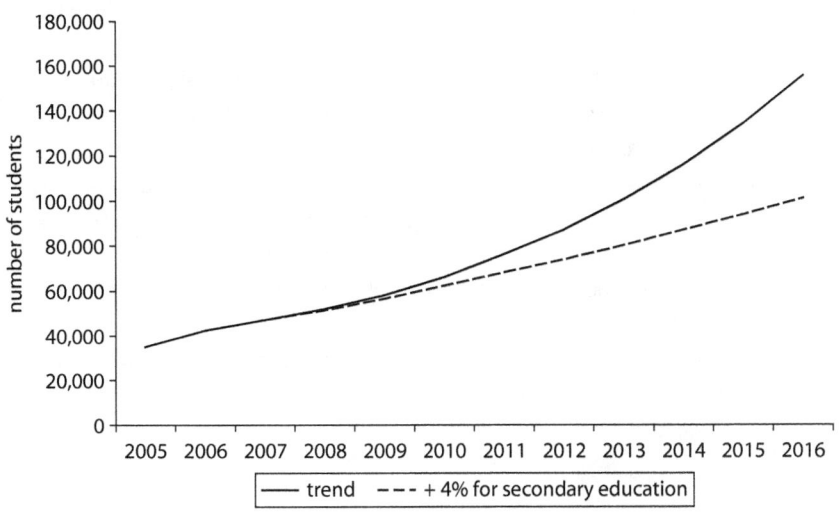

Source: Gioan 2005.

Box 4.6

Selective Admission into Higher Education

Madagascar. To deal with a considerable increase in the number of students, in the early 1990s, Madagascar adopted various measures including selective admission to the university. Admission is based on an examination (particularly for vocational studies) or an evaluation of applications. In 2006, only 54 percent of new *baccalauréat* holders were admitted to a higher education institution. Access to higher education depends largely on the type of *baccalauréat* obtained. By the criteria used, such access is easiest for those with a mathematics *baccalauréat* (96.1 percent admission rate in 2006) and most difficult for those with a literary or technological *baccalauréat* (46.9 percent and 13.8 percent admission rate, respectively; see Madagascar, Ministry of Higher Education and Research 2008).

Kenya. The Joint Admission Board regulates access to public higher education in Kenya through highly selective criteria according to which only candidates with a C+ grade at the end of secondary education are eligible for admission to university. Of those students, approximately 10,000 are allowed to register in a regular university program each year. The remaining candidates may register by paying relatively high tuition fees. In 2004/05, for instance, of 193,087 potential candidates, 58,218 were eligible for admission to the university and only 10,200 were admitted by the Joint Admission Board—namely, 17.5 percent of the eligible candidates (and 5.3 percent of secondary education graduates). These selection procedures ensure a level of (public and private) financing that safeguards the quality of education.

Uganda. Unable to finance the education of all potential higher education candidates, the state takes charge of an annual quota of 4,000 new students, paying their tuition and living costs including room and board, transportation, and health care. The 4,000 quota accounts for only 17 percent of candidates who are eligible based on their "A" level results and 10 percent of candidates who are eligible as a result of their performance on an entrance examination. Since 2005/06, 75 percent of the 4,000 new students are admitted based not only on merit, but also on the relevance of their area of study to national development, with priority given, in particular, to science and technology. This way the state manages to orient student flows toward high-priority areas and to ensure financing of the higher education system.

Sources: Zaafrane 2008; Otieno 2008; Musisi and Mayega 2007.

Reducing the average duration of studies may help to contain the increase in the student population. Contrary to the primary and secondary levels where the legal period of school attendance is the same for all students, the duration of higher education studies may vary considerably. A degree may be obtained in two, three, five, or eight years or may take even longer in some areas of specialization. In addition, students may be required to repeat courses, or they may change disciplines. As a result, it is common for students to attend university for 10, 12, or 14 years. Since the net number of students in the system is a function of annual admissions and departures, the longer the studies, the greater the increase in the number of students attending an institution. The theoretical case shown in figure 4.2 illustrates the impact of a reduction in the average duration of studies on that increase. In this example, given a constant inflow of students and an average 3 or 10-year period of studies, the student population after 15 years would be 42,000 or 105,000 (2.5 times more), respectively.

Figure 4.2   Number of Students as a Function of Length of Studies

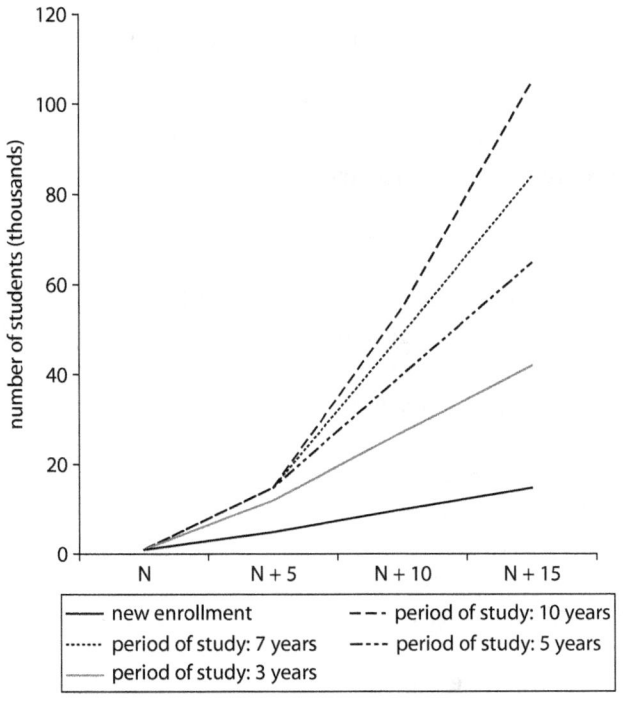

Source: Gioan 2007.

The average period spent by a student to obtain a degree can be reduced by various types of measures, which may be used in combination. Such measures include developing short vocational programs, limiting or prohibiting double repeats (still frequent in many countries from the third year of higher education onward), ensuring computerized monitoring of reenrollments or multiple changes of discipline, introducing selective procedures for admission to the second stage of higher education (namely, the master's level in the LMD structure), making student career paths more fluid by recognizing prior learning, and establishing more selective policies for granting scholarships only to needy students and for specific periods (in the absence of such a policy, students have an incentive to remain in the system, especially if they cannot find employment easily). As the 2005 simulation carried out in Mali shows, using several such measures in combination would make it possible to contain the increase in the number of students. In that example, if one combines regulation in secondary education (a 4 percent annual increase) with the introduction of short vocational programs for approximately 20 percent of the students and the promotion of a private sector that would absorb 20 percent of the students, the projected number of students in 2015 would be only 75,000 instead of 160,000, the level estimated on the basis of the current trend. If one introduces selection at entrance into higher education (a 70 percent rate of access), the number of students would stabilize at 50,000 (see figure 4.3).

Developing Distance Education

Distance education is developing rapidly in all regions of the world, especially thanks to the flexibility that it offers, which allows, among other advantages, the promotion of lifelong education. Under certain conditions, distance education also makes it possible to respond to steep increases in the number of students at a marginal cost significantly lower than that of face-to-face teaching. However, distance education presupposes that the considerable initial investment it requires (particularly for staff training and adaptation of teaching materials) may be depreciated, that student demand materializes, and that electronic connection costs are moderate. In Africa, distance education may contribute to reducing unit costs provided that networks function better and that electronic connection rates fall drastically (see box 4.7).

Mobilizing Private Resources

The issue of cost sharing in higher education is contentious in many African countries. The debate between social and individual benefits is

Figure 4.3 Estimated Number of Higher Education Students in Mali, Assuming Current Trends and Various Flow Management Measures, 2005–16

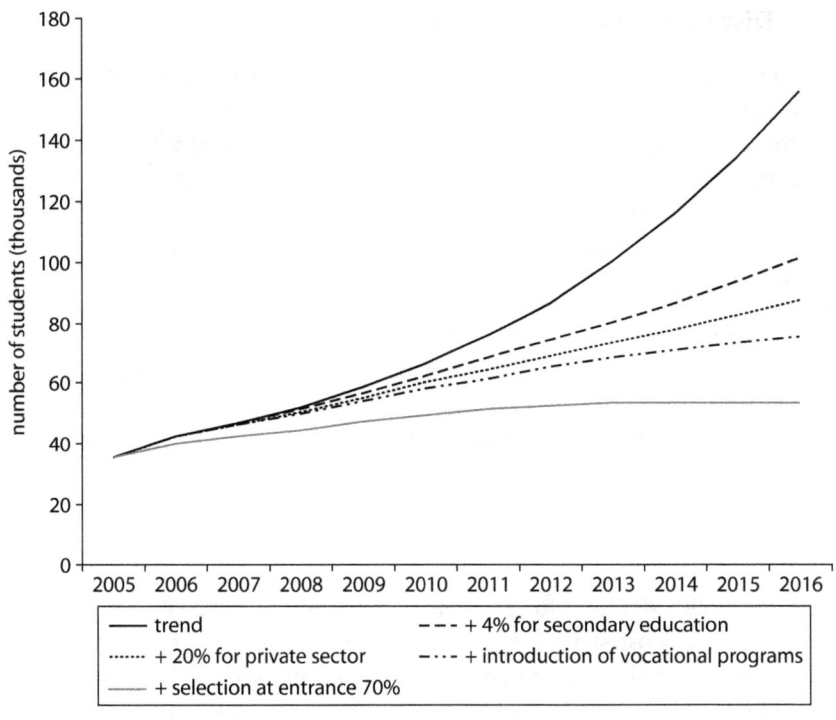

Source: Gioan 2005.

clearly influenced by the particular economic, social, and political conditions at play in each country as well as by its history. If the social benefits of higher education were clear following independence when the priority was to create a base of human resources that could govern the newly independent countries, they are less so at present, when many graduates are unemployed or when the most qualified find the best opportunities in other countries. For many of these graduates, it is clearly a question of individual benefits. Each country should initiate a discussion about the best use of public resources, especially as these are limited and the trade-offs must be a function of national priorities. A successful shift in financial policies toward greater sustained revenue in support of higher education by parents and extended families as well as students requires several steps.

A parental or student contribution toward formerly free housing (that is, a housing fee) can bring as much relief to a strained government budget as a contribution toward instructional costs (that is, a tuition fee). Thus,

> **Box 4.7**
>
> ## A Distance Education Experiment
>
> The International Institute for Water and Environmental Engineering, based in Burkina Faso, has included in its development strategy a distance education course list expected to double the number of students enrolled in the institution in five years. Within weeks, more than 500 applications from 24 countries had been submitted for this program, which leads to a degree. The 2008/09 class—the institute's first—produced 50 graduates. This speedy success is evidence of the following:
>
> - Quality distance education is possible in an African country.
> - This form of education has a customer base, ready in certain cases to pay for its cost.
> - This method may be developed with existing material and human resources.
>
> *Source:* International Institute for Water and Environmental Engineering 2009.

the first policy decision for an African government seriously contemplating additional cost sharing must be whether to feature the introduction of or a substantial increase in a tuition fee as opposed to the introduction of or increase in a food or a housing fee. The reason for separating these two steps is, in part, to avoid too great and too sudden an increase in total costs to students and families. In addition, it is generally thought to be easier both substantively and politically to defend a reduction in subsidies (that is, the introduction of or substantial increase in fees for food and housing) than to introduce tuition fees for the costs of instruction where they did not exist (although the introduction of a small tuition fee at the same time as the introduction of more substantial fees for food and housing might also be politically defensible).

When tuition fees are to be part of the cost-sharing policy, the first decision to be made is whether these fees are to be up-front and expected from parents or extended families (if possible, as determined through means testing) or deferred and expected from students in the form of additional loans (and thus officially not from parents or families). Deferred fees, as in Ethiopia, Lesotho, and Botswana and modeled after schemes in Australia and the United Kingdom, have the advantage of being less obviously a tuition fee (even though they are). Thus, in some circumstances and in some countries, they may be more politically palatable. At the same time, only an expectation of up-front tuition fees ensures that parents and extended families will contribute to these tuition fees (to the limit of official expectations as determined by means testing).

Simultaneously with the advent of (or a substantial increase in) up-front tuition fees, there needs to be a means test to determine either the amount of the officially expected parental or family contribution or simply whether the family is or is not expected to contribute, with the government ready to step in with grants or loans if the family cannot be expected to contribute. Means-testing software programs have been developed in Rwanda, Kenya, and South Africa to determine what individual students can reasonably afford to pay for higher education.

Also simultaneously with the introduction of new fees should be the introduction of or an increase in the size of a student loan scheme for the government to be able to make a credible claim that the introduction of the new fees need not close off higher education opportunities for students from poor families (see box 4.8). The most important features of the student loan scheme—if it is to be part of a policy in the direction of greater cost sharing—are that subsidies be limited, professional collection management be set up to maximize repayments, and provision be made for tapping private capital markets for some of the new student loans. To date, the schemes in Kenya and South Africa remain the most successful as judged by cost-effectiveness and reach.

Cost-Effectiveness of Alternative Forms of Student Financial Assistance

Targeting financial assistance to the most needy requires a fair and cost-effective system for assessing a family's ability to pay for higher education and for providing government assistance to fill in for expected contributions from those families whose income is insufficient. Targeting (or means testing) thus contributes toward greater efficiency (such that the combination of tuition fees plus means-tested financial assistance can target more of the taxpayer assistance where it will make a difference in accessibility) as well as greater equity (in that parents are expected to pay what they can, but with financial assistance for those families who cannot).

Means testing with any degree of fairness and sensitivity is complex, difficult, and costly, especially in developing economies such as those of Sub-Saharan Africa where, except for civil servants and employees of substantial businesses, earnings may be sporadic, frequently unreported, and often shared within a family unit—all of which makes current incomes

> **Box 4.8**
>
> **Phasing the Introduction of Cost Sharing: The Case of Tanzania**
>
> In response to public demand for higher education in the context of scarce public resources, after a period of totally free education, in 1992 the government of Tanzania introduced a cost-sharing policy that expects beneficiaries to contribute gradually to the cost of their training. The policy consists of three main phases:
>
> - *Phase 1 (1992).* Students are required to meet transportation and academic as well as administrative costs.
> - *Phase 2 (1994).* In addition to the requirements of phase 1, this phase plans for living expenses (mostly food and housing) to be covered by the students themselves. For those who cannot afford to meet these costs, repayable loans are available.
> - *Phase 3 (2005).* In addition to the contributions included in phases 1 and 2, students are expected to contribute to education costs. The level of this contribution is set by each institution and should in principle cover the real costs of the training provided. Repayable loans allow students to cover these costs in both public and private institutions. Repayment starts at the completion of studies and is normally spread over a maximum of 10 years, interest free.
>
> *Source:* Thomas and Rawle 2006.

difficult to verify. Thus means-testing systems in South Africa, Kenya, and other countries generally incorporate, in addition to statements of current earnings and documentation of income tax, various categorical indicators that are difficult to disguise and relatively easy and inexpensive to monitor, such as occupation, neighborhood, or type of secondary school in which the children are enrolled, in addition to assets such as a home, livestock, or a car. Thus, categorical indicators along with reported income and other factors are thought to provide more robust indicators of a family's financial ability to contribute toward a child's higher educational expenses (Tekleselassie and Johnstone 2004).

Improvement of the Efficiency and Sustainability of Student Loan Programs

The advantage of student loans that are only minimally subsidized and mostly recovered (that is, with defaults minimized) is that they can at least in theory be a more cost-effective form of financing than targeted aid in that in a context of limited resources, they enable access to a greater number of students. These loans are also much more cost-effective than the same volume of subsidy expended in low– or no–tuition fee formats or in loans or grants that are not targeted. For this reason and in spite of the generally dismal performance of student loan schemes in Sub-Saharan Africa, student loans continue to be an attractive option for countries looking for cost-effective means of financing higher education.

Following are some summary points pertaining to the possible role of student loans in Sub-Saharan Africa. These points are implied by the theory of cost sharing, by the experiences (both positive and negative) of student loan schemes throughout the world, and by the poor record of student lending in Sub-Saharan Africa.

Student loans can—both in theory and in (albeit limited) practice—allow a portion of the costs of instruction or expenses of student living to be shifted to students and repaid when they enter the workforce. Thus, loans can provide additional revenue for the purposes of enhancing capacity, quality, and accessibility in higher education as well as (under some circumstances) the living standards of students.

For a student loan scheme to provide supplementary revenue, two sets of conditions must be met. First, the student loan scheme must lead to additional revenue to accomplish any or all of the purposes suggested above. For a real cost recovery, the loans must have the following characteristics: (a) carry a real, minimally subsidized rate of interest, (b) be collected, and (c) be cost-effectively administered. In other words, the discounted present value of the reasonably anticipated repayment stream—after allowing for some inevitable defaults and other causes of nonrecovery and including financing and administrative costs—must be significantly positive. Second, the student loans—being true assets as long as real repayment streams are made possible by the conditions listed above—must be capitalized, that is, turned into current revenue to achieve the additional capacity, financial assistance, accessibility (by virtue of the aforementioned capacity and financial assistance), or educational quality that justifies the process of cost sharing in the first place. Capitalization thus requires that the loans, presumably made by the government or a government agency, be either sold or securitized.

In addition, if the student loan scheme is to achieve any of the purposes that depend on the ability of the student loans to add resources, the new student contributions—or the discounted present value of the repayment obligation—must genuinely supplement the other sources of financing higher education, namely governments (or taxpayers) and parents (or extended families). Thus, new student contributions, once they have been effectively capitalized (that is, the discounted present value of the repayments made available in the current year), must not substitute either for government subsidies or for reasonable assistance expected from parents or families.

The supplemental revenue made possible by a student loan scheme even at its most effective is limited. If student loans are to be part of a comprehensive package of cost sharing and financial assistance, the loans should be provided in sufficient amounts to cover—at least for a target population—tuition fees plus a minimal amount for student maintenance minus expected family contributions and realistic expectations of part-time and summer earnings. The goal is to provide sufficient lending to make possible higher educational participation without lessening a reasonable expected parental contribution or—where possible—reasonable part-time student employment.

The repayment obligation should be spread over just enough time for the monthly payments to be manageable. Benchmarks should be established as to what constitutes a manageable loan repayment, but a maximum of 10–15 percent of earnings might be a starting point. The fixed schedule of repayments may be scaled to increase over time as an option of the borrower.

If the form of loan is fixed schedule (that is, not contingent on income), the scheduled repayments should be automatically deferrable in the event of unemployment, prolonged illness, loss of employment, or other such demonstrated criteria. Borrowers needing repayment deferment should be placed on an extended repayment schedule, and the monthly repayments should be lowered. Provision should be made to forgive the remaining indebtedness of a borrower after some period of extension beyond the originally scheduled repayment period if he or she is still unable to repay the initial debt at the required rate of interest. Thus, low earners will pay for most of the life of the loan in largely income-contingent form.

Student loans will always be expensive, and a loan scheme should not be launched in the mistaken notion that it will become self-funded (that is, with repayments sufficient to finance all new lending). In fact, all student loan schemes that are generally available are costly to the government. These costs include (a) the costs of necessary guarantees to cover the inherently high risk of default; (b) the cost of subsidies to bring the effective interest rate down below, say, the prevailing rate of consumer debt generally or near to the government's own borrowing rate; (c) the cost of administration, including means testing, origination, and collection; and (d) the costs of debt forgiveness whether such debts are forgiven to encourage academic success or postgraduation behavior or to reflect low lifetime earnings or the failure of the acquired higher education to pay off sufficiently to repay the indebtedness without undue burden.

However, the real reason that constant annual infusions of new lending capital are needed is the inevitable increase over time in the number of new loans stemming from increasing enrollment as well as the increase in the amount of each new loan over time due to rising expenses (due, if for no other reason, to high rates of inflation). In short, there is no way that repayments can ever begin to cover needed new lending.

The generally high rates of default on student loans are the main danger for student loan schemes in any country and are especially pernicious in Sub-Saharan Africa due to several factors, including (a) the absence in most countries of a widespread credit culture that understands the meaning of credit and the obligations that follow, especially outside the middle class in the metropolitan centers; (b) the weakness of the economies and the high rates of unemployment even after college or university graduation; (c) the prevalence of emigration, which further complicates collection; and (d) a resentment of (and resistance to) the entire notion of cost sharing, especially in the Francophone countries, but extending to all of Sub-Saharan Africa (and most of the world). After good lending practices have been secured, such as obligatory exit interviews for student borrowers prior to graduation and connections made between the student loan agency and other government agencies on the whereabouts of borrowers, the risk of default, remains high, should be shared between government and, where possible, family cosignatories. Some cosignatory requirements may need to be limited to an obligation to assist in tracing the borrower and other forms of moral persuasion and will need to be supplemented by additional government guarantees for borrowers who may lack any creditworthy cosignatories.

The origination of the loans should generally be vested in a public corporation that is accountable to (but insulated from) government and its politics as much as possible. In addition, ongoing efforts are needed to educate (as well as listen to) key stakeholders such as government and opposition politicians, top civil servants, students, and the general public on the difficult decisions and complex trade-offs involving higher educational quality, accessibility, and the needs of the society and the economy. Universities and other higher education institutions should also be involved and made responsible for means testing as well as for repayment obligation counseling before borrowers receive their degree. Institutions should bear some financial exposure for excessive defaults.

Promoting the Capacity of Institutions to Diversify their Resources

Diversified financing implies that higher education institutions are capable of generating their own resources. Institutions may generate considerable financial resources by offering attractive vocational education programs whose costs candidates are willing to share provided that they are certain of employment upon completion of the training. Institutions may also develop continuing education programs (whether or not leading to a degree) in which enterprises or individuals are ready to invest. Lastly, they may provide expert or research services. Many universities in Africa are developing these kinds of activities.

Higher education institutions should have sufficient autonomy to develop income-generating activities. They should manage their own budget and use the resources they generate in accordance with their development objectives. Moreover, incentive measures are necessary to mobilize both the actors operating the services in question and the institution. With this aim in view, bases of apportionment should be drawn up for a balanced and equitable redistribution of the resources generated, to the benefit of the university community as a whole. For instance, the University of Parakou in Benin has decided to redistribute revenue from education activities as follows: 60 percent to the income-generating unit, 15 percent to the university's general administration, 5 percent to research, 5 percent to the central university library, and 5 percent to the library of the income-generating unit.

Streamlining Student Support Services

Criteria for allocating direct financial assistance should be in line with equity or efficiency goals. Frequently, these criteria fail to target the neediest students. Nor do they necessarily channel assistance to students in disciplines relevant to national development or take into consideration the respective budgets. In fact, grant and scholarship legislation often does not provide for limits on the number of beneficiaries because such facilities are allocated according to academic criteria rather than the number of places in the universities. In some countries, unless the legislation is amended, there is a risk that the annual cost overruns of scholarships, and other forms of financial aid will accumulate, taking up an increasing part of the higher education budget (see box 4.9).

> **Box 4.9**
>
> ## Some Rules for Avoiding Budget Overruns Resulting from Grants or Scholarships
>
> Two rules for avoiding budget overruns are as follows:
>
> - Define annual allocation quotas for scholarships and grants by type of institution, discipline, and year of study, as a function of government priorities and available budget resources; define allocation criteria that, depending on established allocation policy, include parameters such as academic achievement, age, gender, and family situation; weight each criterion and establish a ranking of candidates each year.
> - Have an impartial and recognized commission (representing all stakeholders and individuals external to the university) allocate grants and scholarships on the basis of the candidates' ranking and the applicable quotas, have scholarships and grants allocated for one academic year, and ensure that every year the number of beneficiaries is a function of the respective annual budget.
>
> *Source:* Authors.

Scholarships abroad should be limited strictly to studies of essential relevance to national development. These scholarships, whose individual amounts are much higher than those of national scholarships, may represent an important part of the higher education budget. Usually, the beneficiaries belong to the most favored social classes, and the rules by which these scholarships are awarded are opaque. If a limit is placed on such scholarships, the resulting savings may be used to build and offer quality local education (see box 4.10).

In some countries, governments have room to rationalize the provision of food, housing, and transportation subsidies. In French-speaking countries, social spending for students often approaches or exceeds 50 percent of total public resources allocated to higher education. In some cases, student food and housing are nonnegotiable items in the social support budget, but benefit a limited number of students. In Benin, for instance, in 2008, student food, housing, and transportation accounted for almost 20 percent of public resources allocated to higher education, while housing and transportation beneficiaries and subsidized housing beneficiaries accounted, respectively, for only 5 percent and 13 percent of students. In view of budget constraints, the considerable weight attached to social spending is a major drag on higher education expansion and quality

Box 4.10

An Alternative to Scholarships Abroad: Building and Offering Quality Local Education

In 2007/08, more than 20 percent of Mauritanian students received a scholarship to study abroad. Those scholarships accounted for 36 percent of the higher education budget. In the case of Guinea-Bissau, that rate in the same period exceeded 80 percent. Part of those public resources may be channeled to supporting—possibly, but not necessarily, through international partnerships—the development of a local (public or private) quality education system attractive to both national and foreign students.

Morocco is a case in point (see fig 4.4). In 2006, Morocco offered more than 40 relocated French university programs, leading to a degree mainly at the master's level, that were of interest to students in Morocco and other countries. In the period 2003–06, the policy of building and offering attractive education translated into a significant increase in the number of foreign students (from 3,000 to 5,000) and a considerable decrease in the number of Moroccans opting to study abroad (from 59,000 to 42,000).

Various reasons can explain these results. African students are attracted by the quality of training in Morocco, which is certified by other foreign universities for a lower cost of living as well as for the proximity to their home countries. The improvement and diversification of the local labor market explain the greater retention of Moroccan students in Morocco.

Figure 4.4 Number of Foreign Students Studying in Morocco and Number of Moroccan Students Studying Abroad, 2003–06

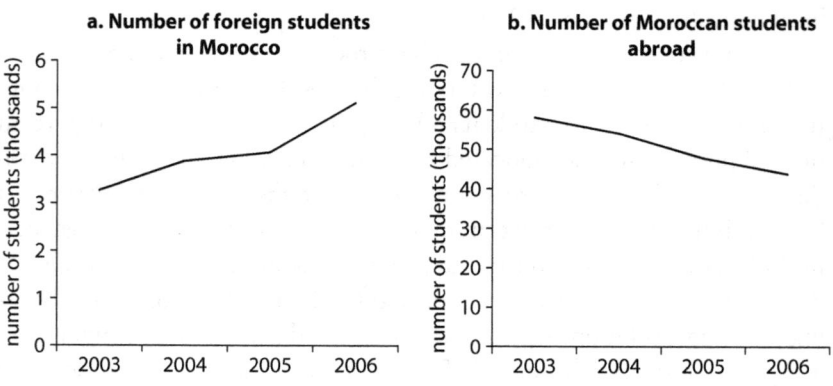

Source: CampusFrance 2008.

improvement. The countries concerned should urgently reverse that trend and rationalize social spending by channeling more public resources toward academic activities and research.

Private-public partnerships could reduce the cost of social benefits without disengaging government from their financing and without sacrificing them. The costs of traditional university housing and catering services are prohibitive, amounting to 5 or 10 times the housing and food costs corresponding to services offered by private operators according to standards closer to local reality. However, involving the private sector in the provision of housing, catering, and transportation services for students requires taking sufficiently attractive measures, constituting, in a way, a risk premium that ensures an adequate return on the investment. Two types of incentives may be envisaged and combined to that purpose: nonfiscal incentives (including land, service infrastructure, development of common areas, various forms of aid, low-interest loans, and partial coverage of rent to arrive at a social cost of rented space and tax incentives for investors and promoters in relation to facility construction, regarding, among others, materials and property and income taxes). Private sector involvement does not mean the total disengagement of the state. In this type of public-private partnership, the state must, in particular, play the role of a facilitator and regulator (setting housing standards, regulating prices, adopting incentive measures, and ensuring follow-up and monitoring). Lastly, as part of the decentralization of university structures, local communities may under certain conditions be entrusted with the implementation of such services (see box 4.11).

Promoting the Private Sector

To the extent that there is an adequate regulatory framework, the development of the private sector may help to diversify higher education and absorb part of the increase in the number of students. Regarding short vocational programs in particular, budget audits conducted in various countries such as Côte d'Ivoire in the early 1990s showed that unit costs in private institutions were often much lower than those in public institutions (by a factor ranging up to 10). Moreover, certain types of highly specialized training, potentially essential to the national economy, do not exist and would be too expensive to launch in the public sector. In such cases, public authorities would be well advised to encourage students to take private sector courses. To that end, scholarships or loans may be granted to a number of students. As motivation for private promoters to invest in higher education, fiscal incentives (including a tax system

> **Box 4.11**
>
> **Examples of the State's Disengagement from Housing, Catering, and Other Nonacademic Services Provided to Students**
>
> A 2005 study conducted in Burkina Faso shows that a student housing program financed mainly by small private promoters would result in a significant gain for the state even if the latter renounced tax revenue and contributed to the investment by providing land to the private promoters and by subsidizing the cost of renting (a net gain on the order of US$160 million on investment and operational expenses over 10 years for a program designed to house 35 percent of the students). The study shows that the cost of student halls managed by the state is four times higher on average than the cost of an equivalent privately managed lodging facility (Gioan and Recamier 2005).
>
> In Côte d'Ivoire, innovative experiments have been tried with a view to involving small private operators in student catering without the state's financial participation. To that end, areas have been developed (with water and power supply and sewage) at, for instance, the public University of Abobo-Adjamé, where private operators set up facilities complying with technical specifications drawn up by the university administration. These specifications may include a standard installation layout, the services authorized, opening hours, quality standards, and the obligation to provide at least one dish at the minimum price charged in a traditional university restaurant. In such cases, the role of public authorities consists essentially of defining the framework of operation and ensuring compliance with the technical specifications.
>
> In Tanzania, the University of Dar es Salaam has reduced costs by contracting out catering services to a number of private providers.
>
> *Source:* PA Gioan.

favorable to establishments recognized as public interest entities and lower customs duties), nonfiscal benefits (including availability of land, buildings, and loans), or national accreditation of degrees are often necessary. These various incentives must be accompanied by a regulatory framework enabling the state to monitor the development of private education and enhance the sector's credibility by imposing requirements, particularly in respect of the quality of instruction and graduation standards. If transparent, such a contractual approach involving the state and private higher education institutions and combining incentives and conditions may have some positive effects. In fact, the fees of private institutions would tend to decline thanks to the incentives provided, allowing for lower registration fees and attracting more students. In that case, the development of the private sector could efficiently supplement public education and allow for a more adequate response to growing demand.

Although the private sector may provide a response to the demand for higher education, governments should ask the following questions: (a) In what disciplines does the private sector provide a cost-effective alternative to the public sector? (b) What accreditation and certification mechanisms should be established to ensure the quality of the services offered? (c) Is help offered to disadvantaged students to attend a private higher education establishment justified on the grounds of equity? and (d) How should an environment conducive to investment in the private sector be created? See box 4.12.

Box 4.12

Development of Private Higher Education in Some African Countries

Inexistent in the early 1990s, Côte d'Ivoire's private higher education subsector has experienced considerable growth, encouraged by the public authorities. To diversify access to higher education, reduce demographic pressure on public university admissions, and promote short vocational programs such as the one leading to the *brevet de technicien supérieur* (advanced technical certificate) at costs lower than those incurred at public institutions, the government has developed a subsidization policy that covers tuition fees. This type of public assistance was designed to encourage the formation of private initiatives, which eventually would constitute a viable alternative to the public sector. After approximately seven years, 30 percent of students were attending a private higher education establishment. Although such government assistance initially provided 100 percent of the revenues of the private institutions in question, students who pay for their tuition have, after more than five years, come to account for more than 40 percent of the student population (in 2008, there were 153 private *grandes écoles* and 11 private universities, located in 18 cities).

In Burundi, the private sector, assisted by the government, which grants scholarships to 25 percent of the students attending private institutions, has grown considerably, accounting for 53 percent of higher education students in 2008.

(continued)

Box 4.12 *(continued)*

In English- and Portuguese-speaking countries, governments have promoted the development of private institutions through enabling legislation such as the Higher Education Proclamation issued by the Ethiopian Parliament in 2003 as well as through various types of financial support. This support is mainly provided indirectly by allowing students to use their government-provided financial assistance to attend private institutions. Since 2007, the government of Botswana has extended scholarships to local students admitted to domestic private institutions. These scholarships take the form of tuition payments by the government for sponsored students (see Pillay 2008). In Kenya and Tanzania, private institution students are eligible for student loans. In Mozambique, the Provincial Scholarship Fund provides support to students in both public and private higher education. A few governments provide direct financial support to private institutions. The Mozambique government uses its quality enhancement and innovation fund to finance both private and public higher education institutions.

Source: Authors.

Rethinking Research Funding

The challenge for African countries is to find ways to sustain the costs of establishing high-quality research institutions. As government budgets are already stretched thinly over many sectors, other options need to be found. One way of coping with the resource constraints is to partner universities with research institutes within and outside the country for the conduct of research, thereby leveraging access to equipment, all the while building valuable relationships between universities and research organizations in both the public and the private sectors (World Bank 2006). This is fundamental to the creation of an enticing research environment that draws industry partners into a mutually beneficial research and development arrangement, as for example, has been the case in the East Asian knowledge economies and elsewhere in the developed world.

For maximization of the economic rate of return, research and education should be aligned to national needs. Access to credible, independent science and technology research aligned to national needs would help to develop informed policies for stimulating economic growth, mitigating environmental problems, adopting new technologies, and responding quickly to outbreaks of new diseases (InterAcademy Council 2004).

Based on experience from international multilateral organizations including the World Bank, some useful lessons have emerged on promoting funding research in developing countries:[5] (a) innovation funds are seen as highly effective mechanisms for boosting educational quality and relevance within participating institutions; (b) national policy goals and institutional strategic priorities should be the main points of reference in the design of innovation funds, and a range of end users and stakeholders should be involved in project design to ensure that this happens; and (c) the role of private institutions in relation to innovation fund activities must be explicitly considered, bearing in mind that enabling private institutions to compete for innovation fund resources generally reinforces the goals of government tertiary education policy with regard to quality, relevance, expanded access, and efficiency (World Bank 2009).

Combining Tools for Financially Sustainable Tertiary Education Policies

The formulation and implementation of new policies must be based first and foremost on the evaluation of short- and long-term needs. Depending on the conditions and constraints proper to each country, various measures—such as reorientation of student flows, cost sharing, rationalization of social expenses, improvement of governance and management practices, and private sector development—may be used in combination to achieve an optimal balance between economic requirements, social needs, political imperatives, quality considerations, and the financial resources that may be mobilized.

Solutions for a sustainable financing of higher education systems exist, provided a strategic medium-term approach is developed and backed by adequate and sustainable resources. To that purpose, decision makers responsible for the development of higher education should consider taking proactive action consisting of the following:

- Analyzing, aimed at identifying the characteristics and trends of their higher education system and the range of possible measures
- Forecasting, aimed at assessing the impact of any changes or reforms envisaged
- Explaining, aimed at illustrating the stakes and the risks involved in not making decisions

- Negotiating, aimed at taking into account the stakeholders' goals and showing convincingly that the proposed trade-offs are well founded and necessary
- Deciding, aimed at implementing the new policies and strategies
- Implementing the changes and monitoring, aimed at ensuring that plans of action are carried out in accordance with the adopted guidelines.

Table 4.2 summarizes the tools that governments can use to design realistic, quality, and financially sustainable higher education policies. Some of the measures, in particular those related to improved management, cost optimization, and distance education, are technically difficult and can require technical assistance from external partners. The rationalization of

Table 4.2   Measures for the Sustainable Financing of Higher Education

Measures	Technical difficulty	Political difficulty	Cost of implementing the measure
Strengthen the auonomy of institutions	+	+	+
Institute institutional assessment procedues	++	++	+
Impose a limit on the duration of scholarships	0	+	0
Establish a distance education system	++	0	++
Monitor the use of expenditure	+	+	+
Mobilize external assistance through the formulation of a medium-term strategy	++	0	+
Share education costs by the beneficiaries	0	++	0
Raise the level of institutions' own resources	+	0	+
Establish competitive grant schemes	+	0	+
Establish student loans	+	0	++

Source: Authors.
Note: 0 = no particular difficulty or financial cost in relation to implementation of the measure; + = average difficulties and costs in relation to implementation of the measure; ++ = significant difficulties and costs in relation to implementation of the measure.

resources and the promotion of the autonomy of higher education institutions are sensitive topics and can face political and or social resistance. They indeed can change some habits for both teaching staff and students. Other measures such as restricting access, limiting social benefits or services to students, or implementing cost-sharing policies are not technically difficult, but can present political challenges. Each country needs to combine different options or tools, depending on its singular situation, its social environment, and the political will of its leaders, to best respond to the need of the population for higher education.

Notes

1. As pressure for cost sharing in higher education intensifies, especially in Francophone countries, better mechanisms will be needed for projecting costs, budgeting expenditures, and managing finances.
2. However, the performance contract is not a solitary instrument for higher education reform. Because performance contracts cover multiyear periods, usually three to five years, government must have in hand a strategic vision for the sector's development to guide the design and negotiation of performance contracts within a perspective of program budgeting.
3. According to UNESCO, BREDA (2007), the countries with the lowest rates of access to secondary education in 2000 have since been characterized by average annual increase rates higher than 10 percent as a result of improved primary school enrollment.
4. The rate was calculated as an average for 35 countries for which data were available (UNESCO, BREDA 2007). In 10 of those countries, the rate was less than 2 percent.
5. Since 1992, the World Bank has financed competitive funding to improve tertiary education and research in 29 projects benefiting 23 countries.

References

Adu, Kingsley, and François Orivel. 2006. *Tertiary Education Funding Strategy in Ghana*. Accra: Ministry of Education, Sports, and Culture.

Atuahene, Francis. 2008. "Higher Education Finance in Ghana." *International Higher Education* 50 (winter): 20–21.

Brouwer, R., A. Pimpão, M. Souto, and M. Valente. 2008. *Analysis of the Impact of the Quality Enhancement and Innovation Fund*. Maputo: Ministry of Education.

CampusFrance. 2008. *Student Mobility: Three Geographical Examples*. Paris: CampusFrance.

Gioan, Pierre Antoine. 1995. "Enseignement supérieur en Côte d'Ivoire: Trois années de réformes." Unpublished manuscript. Agence EduFrance, Paris.

———. 2005. "Republic of Mali: Study Relating to the Formulation of Guidelines for National Policy on Higher Education and Research." Agence EduFrance, Paris.

———. 2007. "Higher Education in French-Speaking Africa: What Levers for Financially Sustainable Policies?" Working Paper 13, World Bank, Washington, DC.

Gioan, Pierre Antoine, and Philippe Recamier. 2005. *Etude relative à la formulation d'une politique de logements pour étudiants impliquant le secteur privé*. Paris: United Nations Educational, Scientific, and Cultural Organization.

InterAcademy Council. 2004. "Inventing a Better Future." InterAcademy Council, Amsterdam. http://www.interacademycouncil.net/?id=10011.

International Institute for Water and Environmental Engineering. 2009. "Formation ouverte et à distance du 2IE." International Institute for Water and Environmental Engineering, Burkina Faso. http://www.FOAD-2IE-edu.org.

Madagascar, Ministry of Higher Education and Research. 2008. *Study on the Costs of Higher Education*. Antananarivo: Ministry of Higher Education and Research.

Musisi, N. B., and F. N. Mayega. 2007. *Access and Equity in Higher Education: Assessing Financing Policies; A Comparative Study of African Countries—Uganda*. Kampala: Makerere Institute of Social Research.

Ng'ethe, Njuguna, George Subotzky, and George Afeti. 2008. "Differentiation and Articulation in Tertiary Education Systems: A Study of Twelve African Countries." Education Working Paper 145, World Bank, Washington, DC.

Orr, Dominic. 2005. "Can Performance-based Funding and Quality Assurance Solve the State vs. Market Conundrum?" *Higher Education Policy* 18 (1): 31–50.

Otieno, Wycliffe. 2008. *Access and Equity in Higher Education: Assessing Financing Policies in Kenya*. Washington, DC: Partnership for Higher Education in Africa.

Pillay, Pundy. 2008. "Higher Education Funding Frameworks in SADC." In *Towards a Common Future: Higher Education in the SADC Region; Research Findings from Four SARUA Studies*, ed. Piyushi Kotecha. Johannesburg: Southern African Regional Universities Association.

Saint, William. 2006. "Innovation Funds for Higher Education: A Users' Guide for World Bank–Funded Projects." Education Working Paper 1, World Bank, Washington, DC.

Salmi, Jamil, and Arthur M. Hauptman. 2006. "Innovations in Tertiary Education Financing: A Comparative Evaluation of Allocation Mechanisms." Education Working Paper 4, World Bank, Washington, DC.

Tekleselassie, Abebayehu, and D. Bruce Johnstone. 2004. "Means Testing: The Dilemma of Targeting Subsidies in African Higher Education." *Journal of Higher Education in Africa* 2 (2): 135–58.

Thomas, H., and Georgina Rawle. 2006. *Tanzania Higher and Technical Education Subsector Cost and Financing Study*. Oxford: Oxford Policy Management.

UNESCO (United Nations Educational, Scientific, and Cultural Organization), BREDA (Bureau for Education in Africa). 2007. *Education pour tous en Afrique: L'urgence de politiques sectorielles intégrées*. Dakar: UNESCO, BREDA.

World Bank. 2002. *Constructing Knowledge Societies: New Challenges for Tertiary Education*. Washington, DC: World Bank.

———. 2006. "Nigeria, Science and Technology Education at Post-basic Level (STEPB): Review of S&T Education in Federally Funded Institutions." Africa Region Human Development Department, World Bank, Washington, DC.

———. 2009. "Project Information Document in Higher Education Science and Technology: Mozambique." World Bank, Washington, DC.

Zaafrane, H. 2008. *Etude sur les coûts et le financement de l'enseignement supérieur à Madagascar*. Antananarivo: Ministère de l'Education Nationale et de la Recherche Scientifique.

CHAPTER 5

Ensuring the Successful Implementation of Financing Reforms

Financing reforms are without doubt among the most challenging policy changes that governments face. Governments may not have the political will to introduce radical change, stakeholders may be opposed to the proposed reforms, and institutions may not have the managerial capacity to operate in a more efficient and flexible way. Cost sharing, cost containment, resource diversification, reduction in subsidies to students, and changes in budget allocation mechanisms are contentious topics. International experience shows that the launch and implementation of tertiary education reforms have a higher probability of success when decision makers manage to assess effectively the contexts of the reform environment, to build a consensus among the various constituents of the tertiary education community, to mobilize additional resources to provide tangible incentives in support of the reform, to strengthen the incentive framework through appropriate changes in the governance structure and arrangements, to bolster planning and management capacities at the systemwide and institutional levels, and to anticipate unintended consequences.

Addressing the Political Feasibility of Reforms

As Machiavelli wrote in his famous political manifesto, *The Prince*, "There is nothing more difficult to take in hand, more perilous to conduct, or more uncertain in its success than to take the lead in introducing a new order of things." While this observation is true of any political reform, it is particularly resonant in the case of tertiary education reforms. Universities are among the most conservative cultural and organizational institutions, with extremely vocal yet highly transitory constituencies, including faculty and students. These groups can effectively mobilize themselves against policy changes likely to challenge established practices and vested interests. This is often the case when it comes to financing reforms such as the introduction of tuition fees, the reduction in social benefits for students, the elaboration of a transparent funding formula for public resource allocation, or the amalgamation of existing tertiary education institutions to achieve economies of scale.

Not enough attention is paid to the political economy of tertiary education reforms on the assumption that a technically sound reform program is all that is needed for change to succeed. But when it comes to implementation, political reality invariably proves stronger than the technocratic vision. For instance, in 1999 students in Germany organized the largest demonstrations in Europe since the 1960s to protest deteriorating conditions in the universities (lack of funding, overcrowded lecture halls, length of time needed to graduate) and to demand more funding for tertiary education (Altbach 1999). In Mexico, the 270,000 students at the National Autonomous University of Mexico (UNAM), the country's flagship university, went on strike in March 1999 after the university council approved a plan to raise tuition for the first time in more than 50 years from the equivalent of about US$0.02 per semester to US$70.00. After six weeks, the rector yielded and announced that the fees would be paid on a voluntary basis only; the students continued the strike and occupied the university. UNAM remained closed for 10 months until the police eventually expelled the strikers. In France, both teacher and student unions have vehemently opposed the governance reform announced by the government in 2008, which aims to give more autonomy to universities while reinforcing the powers of university presidents. The students went on strike and occupied some universities. Whether the reform will be implemented remains to be seen.

Similarly, in many African countries, interest groups have often resisted proposed reform programs or actively protested against unsatisfactory study and living conditions. In 1991, in Mali a crowd of angry students killed the minister of education. When the government of Kenya introduced fees in 1992, a riot broke out, and a student was killed. In December 2001, police killed two students in the Democratic Republic of Congo during a demonstration against tuition fees. Again in Mali, students angry over the lack of government support for higher education threatened to disrupt the African Soccer Cup in January 2002. When the utility company cut electricity to the student dormitories at the University of Antananarivo in May 2007 because the university had not paid its bills, angry Malagasy students blocked the road to the airport until the government agreed to pay on behalf of the university.

Therefore, to avoid or at least minimize possible failure, decision makers need to deal carefully with the political sensitivity of the financing reforms under consideration. This involves four fundamental elements. The first one is a social assessment of the proposed reform to review the needs and preoccupations of all major stakeholders. This starts with an analysis of the tertiary education environment with the purpose of identifying all interst groups by asking the following questions: among all those identified, (a) Who stands to gain and who stands to lose from the proposed reform? (b) Who benefits in the existing system? (c) Who will benefit in the new system? and (d) Who is likely to be indifferent, supportive, or dissenting?

This type of analysis and assessment allows for distinguishing between those groups that may be positively concerned by the proposed reforms and those that are likely to lose privileges or be negatively affected by changes in existing financing modalities and practices. With the results of the social assessment in hand, government authorities can more easily identify potential champions who can be relied on to play a leading part in implementation of the reform. They can also conduct a risk analysis to better anticipate reactions in the camp of potential "losers."

The second and perhaps more crucial step is the consensus-building phase (see box 5.1). Translating a reform program into reality depends to a large extent on the ability of decision makers to use the social assessment tool to build consensus among the diverse constituents of the tertiary education community, allowing for a high degree of tolerance for controversies and disagreements. A potentially effective approach for addressing the political sensitivity of the proposed reforms is to initiate a wide consultation process concerning the need for and content of the envisaged changes. The purpose of consensus-building activities is to make all stakeholders aware of the linkage between the proposed reforms

> **Box 5.1**
>
> **Consensus Building and Cost Sharing in Northern Mexico**
>
> The Mexican constitution provides for free public education at all levels, and cost sharing has always been fiercely resisted by both professors and students at UNAM. In northern Mexico, by contrast, the rector of the public University of Sonora was successful in introducing cost sharing after initiating a consensus-building process in 1993 to explain to the staff and students the need for supplementary resources to maintain the quality of teaching and learning.
>
> After some initial resistance, including a widely publicized 2,000-kilometer march by protesters from Hermosillo to Mexico City, the students accepted the principle of a yearly payment to generate supplementary resources. A participatory process was initiated to determine the allocation of these resources to equity and quality improvement initiatives. Since 1994, the students have been paying an annual contribution of about US$300 for this purpose. A joint student-faculty committee administers the funds, which are used to provide scholarships for low-income students, renovate classrooms, upgrade computer labs, and purchase scientific textbooks and journals. A poster is prepared every year to disseminate information on the use of the money collected at the beginning of the academic year.
>
> *Source:* World Bank 2002.

and the likely improvements that they could bring about in teaching and learning conditions. As illustrated by the experience of Mozambique, this effort involves a blend of rational analysis, political maneuvering, and psychological interplay to bring all of the concerned stakeholders on board.

After emerging from a crippling civil war in 1992, Mozambique realized that its vast potential wealth could only be unlocked by sharply increasing the number of its young people graduating from tertiary education. The country decided to double its investment in education. It initiated a comprehensive tertiary education reform and proceeded to organize countrywide consultations to seek input from academics, students, business people, and nongovernmental organizations. In May and June 2000, the minister in charge of the newly established Ministry of Higher Education, Science, and Technology, organized regional consultations at which she and her colleagues held separate sessions with people from each of Mozambique's 10 provinces. About 10 people came from each province, representing existing higher education institutions, students, businesses, regional government, and civic associations. Each province was asked to prepare its own development plan, including its training needs. Of course, the provinces asked for much more than there were resources to fund. But the consultations helped the ministry to attain its goal of planning a rational—and equitable—use of available resources.

The consultations built a broad base of support for the reforms and helped the minister to identify "champions" for change. "Champions need to be identified and encouraged at all levels," she says. "Champions are people who are interested in the process, who can bring knowledge to it, and who are able to mobilize others around the vision." The results of the regional consultations were presented in July 2000 to a national seminar with 300 participants from all the provinces, higher education institutions, government ministries, and Parliament. Out of this gathering came the Strategic Plan for Higher Education in Mozambique 2000–10, which was approved by the government's Council of Ministers the following month (Bollag 2003).

Obviously, consensus building is not a magic formula that will guarantee success each time. Involving potential opponents in the policy discussion carries risks. In South Africa, for instance, implementation of the tertiary education reform announced in February 2001—the culmination of four years of national consultations involving wide political debates based on the initial work of expert committees—was stalled by the political resistance of some constituencies. Yet ignoring potential opponents and failing to engage them in a dialogue about the proposed reforms is a recipe for failure.

A key third ingredient for facilitating acceptance of reforms that challenge the status quo is the availability of additional resources that can be channeled toward tertiary education institutions and other concerned groups such as students. This can help to transform what could be called an "undoing reform" into a "constructing" reform. For example, the positive reaction that followed the reforms introduced by the Higher Education Commission in Pakistan in the past few years, including the new funding formula and the performance-based tenure track, was due in large part to the fact that the budget for tertiary education has more than doubled since 2002. Similarly, in Chile the establishment in 2006 of a new student loan program allowing low-income students to enroll in private universities and institutes was met with a favorable reception. In the Côte d'Ivoire, the government was able to win acceptance for low tuition fees—around US$100 a year—by committing to allocating a portion of the revenues generated by these fees to subsidizing the student union.

In the same vein, the expansion of tertiary education opportunities through the growth of private institutions can be greatly enhanced by the availability of financial incentives in the form of scholarships and student loans. It is significant that the four African nations where private enrollment in tertiary education has soared (Botswana, Burundi, Côte d'Ivoire, and Mozambique) are among the few countries where the government does not restrict scholarships to students at public institutions only.

Another way to increase political acceptability and avoid disruptions is to introduce "grandfather" provisions and transitory funding arrangements guaranteeing that all institutions and beneficiary groups receive amounts of resources equal to those they would have received under the previous system, at least for some period of time. Pakistan's newly designed funding formula, for example, replaced the traditional negotiated budget system and had an equalization component to compensate for past disparities in budget allocations. To avoid antagonizing the more powerful universities that would experience the greatest changes under the new formula, the equalization part of the formula Pakistan applied only to the additional resources during the first two years (2004–05). As of 2006, however, the new funding formula was used to calculate the entire budget allocation. Unfortunately, this gradual approach did not work in the case of UNAM in Mexico. Although the proposed fee increase affected only incoming students, the entire student community successfully mobilized itself against the proposed measure.

Similarly, to reduce resistance to change, policy makers can implement financing reforms only with new institutions rather than affecting existing universities. In Mauritius, when the new technology university was established in 2003, incoming students had to pay hefty tuition fees of about US$3,000 a year, whereas students at the University of Mauritius, the country's main public tertiary education institution, pay no tuition. The government expected a positive demonstration effect when the students compared the difference in learning resources across the two universities.

Finally, the fourth and final element is the importance of implementing these reforms in stages and in the proper sequence is important. When the Ghanaian vice chancellors announced a plan to raise tuition fees in public universities in January 2005, they presented it in the form of a 10-year graduated increase program, which facilitated acceptance by the students. Sometimes it is more effective to delay a critical decision by a few weeks or even months to allow sufficient time to build a consensus. In Kenya, for instance, the government tried to raise tuition fees in the early 1990s without any consultation process. This resulted in massive riots, with the sad consequences of a student being killed by the police. Later in the process, the Ministry of Education's reform implementation team sent a letter to the families of students explaining the reasons for introducing tuition fees. This communication effort was instrumental in securing acceptance for the proposed policy change.

Putting in Place Favorable Governance Arrangements

Financing reforms do not happen in an institutional and regulatory vacuum. The ability of governments and tertiary education institutions to implement significant changes in resource mobilization, allocation, and utilization is often constrained by rigid governance structures and processes.

This is especially true in Francophone Sub-Saharan Africa, where most tertiary education systems patterned after the French model are characterized by a mix of control and autonomy features that make it difficult to undertake meaningful transformation. On the one hand, public universities usually enjoy total academic freedom, full independence in the selection of their leaders (by election), and complete management autonomy regarding their daily operations. On the other hand, the government centrally controls key parameters affecting the mode of operation and sustainable financing of public tertiary education institutions, such as the level of their budgetary resources, salary conditions, number of faculty positions, number of incoming students, regulations concerning scholarships, and approval of new programs. These controls undermine the ability of university rectors to manage their institutions effectively, let alone innovatively. Similarly, governance arrangements at the institutional level leave much to be desired. University boards are weak and have limited external representation. The democratic election of university presidents does not guarantee the appointment of professionally qualified leaders, and management practices are outdated.

Putting in place favorable governance arrangements is therefore a key condition of successful financing reforms. This implies granting more management autonomy to public tertiary education institutions. In return, clear performance objectives and channels and levels of accountability should be defined and agreed with the leaders of these institutions. This performance can be monitored through the evaluation-accreditation system in countries where one exists and stimulated by allocation mechanisms linking funding to performance outcomes.

To illustrate in a concrete manner how changes in governance can facilitate financial management, table 5.1 presents the reforms that are under consideration in Madagascar and outlines the main changes that would occur in the context of granting more autonomy to public tertiary education institutions.

Modifying the mode of appointment of the university leaders and the role and configuration of university boards can also help to promote financing reforms. Across the world, more and more countries are setting up external boards with extensive powers over the management of universities. Boards can be responsible for overseeing all aspects of financial management, selecting the president and rector, determining the appointment and employment conditions of staff, and deciding on the management of university property. A recent survey of governance reforms in Sub-Saharan Africa found several countries moving toward greater external representation on university boards, including Botswana, Lesotho, Mauritius, Mozambique, Uganda, and Zambia (Lao and Saint 2009).

Table 5.1 Changing Approaches to Financial Control in Madagascar

Topic	Centralized control	Full autonomy
Annual budgets	Agreed to in detail by the Ministry of Education (MOE) or the funding body	Agreed to by the board (but reported to MOE or the buffer body)
Expenditure	Line item control so that institutions cannot switch expenditure between set budget categories	Freedom to allocate and spend as required within the overall budget awarded by the MOE
Underspending at the end of accounting period	Surrender of underspent sums to MOE or the Ministry of Finance	Freedom to carry forward underspending (and to absorb any overspending from future funds within limits)
External earnings from nongovernment sources	Risk of reduced budget from Ministry of Finance or MOE as a result of perception of additional external earnings	Freedom to retain and spend freely all sums earned from nongovernment sources
Tuition fees for domestic local, domestic out-of-state, and international students	Inability to charge fees for regular programs	Freedom to set fee levels and retain the money without affecting the budget allocation from the government

Source: Salmi 2008.

Even in Francophone systems, these types of reforms are not considered too alien, as the positive experience of Madagascar's two technology institutes and the School of Business Administration (INSCAE) shows (see box 5.2). Unlike the public universities in that country, the technology institutes are able to manage their budgets in an autonomous manner, they rely on contractual teachers to complement their faculty contingent, they control their physical space, and they receive guidance from a dynamic board with external representation. Similarly, INSCAE operates very differently from the public universities. It charges tuition

---

Box 5.2

Autonomy and Excellence at Work: The National School of Business Administration

INSCAE is Madagascar's premier school of business administration. It operates under the authority of the Ministry of Finance, with a special status that gives it real autonomy. The students pay significant annual tuition fees, from $350 for undergraduates to $650 at the graduate level. Professors are remunerated on the basis of a competitive salary scale that recognizes not only academic qualifications but also relevant professional experience. They enjoy additional social benefits and have the opportunity to participate in the school's income generation activities (consulting and executive development courses).

The school is managed like a corporation and subject to external audits. The director is nominated by the government after a competitive search organized by the board. The 11-member board has only three government representatives and five external stakeholder representatives.

The school has a strong culture of quality. Professors are evaluated by the students, their peers, and their supervisors. Nonperforming professors can be dismissed. Unlike most other Malagasy tertiary education institutions, INSCAE organizes its programs in modular fashion and uses the academic credit system. In each discipline, the best student at the end of each term has his or her tuition fees reimbursed. INSCAE is among the first Malagasy institutions to adopt the *licence-master-doctorat* (LMD) structure.

INSCAE has enjoyed excellent results, as demonstrated by the take-up of its graduates among public enterprises and private sector firms. Its financial strength has allowed for high-quality infrastructure and faculty.

Source: Salmi 2008.

fees, links the remuneration and promotion of professors to performance, and enjoys the guidance of a board with a majority of nongovernment representatives.

Finally, strengthening governance and institutional frameworks can help to ensure the sustainability of financing reforms and protect them from political changes. The minister of higher education in Mozambique in the early 2000s established an independent Higher Education Council as a new form of governance instrument that has survived subsequent attempts to weaken the role of the Ministry of Higher Education, Science, and Technology because of its independence as a statutory organization.

Strengthening Planning and Management Capacity

Another key implementation issue is whether governments and tertiary institutions have the capacity to administer the new policies that are enacted. This question of administrative capacity covers a broad range of issues including the ability to conduct effective strategic planning at the national and institutional levels, the capacity to implement modern financial management procedures, the size and experience of staff in managing the proposed changes, and the capacity to collect and process accurate data for management and monitoring purposes. The first tertiary education project supported by the World Bank in Mozambique in the early 1990s included an institutional development component to reinforce the managerial capacities of Eduardo Mondlane University in Maputo. This enabled the university to conduct an 18-month strategic planning effort that established objectives and priorities for the institution's long-term development and was useful for focusing donor assistance in an effective way.

With regard to funding institutional activities, historically based budgets that are negotiated between government and institutional leaders are not only the most traditional way of paying for recurrent expenses and capital investment, but also the type of allocation mechanism that is easiest to implement. By contrast, funding formulas require greater administrative capacity in large part because they rely on accurate data to produce the appropriate allocation figures. For example, it is not advisable for a country to move to a formula based on actual costs per student if those cost figures are not regularly collected or verifiable. Formulas based on average costs or normative costs tend to be easier to manage because they do not require as much detailed information from institutions as actual cost figures.

In general, the availability of appropriate data is a critical element for success of any performance-based allocation mechanism. In Argentina, for example, when the government started to reform the tertiary education system after 1995 and attempted to move to a funding formula, audits revealed that several universities had inflated their enrollment figures to receive more funding. In the following years, a comprehensive management information system was designed and introduced within the context of a World Bank–supported project to provide the entire university system and the government with adequate and reliable information for monitoring progress in implementation of the reform. This has brought about a culture of transparency embedded in more rational resource allocation mechanisms (funding formula and competitive grants).

Similarly, the administrative capacity of governments and institutions is a critical variable in determining the potential success of grant, scholarship, and loan schemes that involve payments to students. For instance, student loan agencies must have the capacity to calculate and monitor the debt accumulated by their student clients. However, governments often consider student loan agencies only as an instrument of social policy and underestimate the need for strong financial management capacity. In the República Bolivariana de Venezuela, for example, during the years of transition from a grant to a student loan agency in the early 1990s, the Student Loan Foundation did not have a financial management system capable of informing graduates returning from their studies overseas of how much they owed. Many graduates saw their loans "forgiven" as a result.

A second, critical determinant of successful implementation of student loan schemes is to use repayment mechanisms that best fit the administrative capacity of the country. Thus, few African countries meet the criteria for successful implementation of income-contingent repayment of student loans, including a comprehensive, efficient, and reliable taxation system or social security system to collect payments. This is likely to be a challenge for the few such schemes that exist today, notably in Botswana, Ethiopia, and Lesotho.

One of the policy questions frequently raised during implementation of student aid programs is the capacity to determine a student's and family's ability to pay for tertiary education. Should the process be a simple one, asking only a few questions to determine family resource levels, or should the determination of eligibility for student aid be a more complicated process, trying to make sophisticated distinctions among families as a means to achieve greater equity in the distribution of financial aid through better targeting (Salmi and Hauptman 2006)?

Building the capacity to define eligibility for student aid in an objective and transparent manner is an important question that policy makers in many African countries need to address in a systematic way. In the absence of income verification measures in countries with a weak taxation system and a dominant informal economy, it is very difficult to obtain reliable and verifiable income data. The targeting options range from administering a simple system, in which a few key verifiable questions are asked of students and their families, to much more complex systems, in which application forms can consist of many pages and detailed instructions. Examples of simple proxy questions include what high school the student attended (especially if schools are ranked by the socioeconomic profile of their students or if a significant proportion of students are enrolled in private institutions), where the student lives, whether the family owns a car or has indoor plumbing, or even the size of the family's electricity bill. Some Catholic universities in the Philippines have used a complex system on the assumption that only needy students would be motivated enough to go through the time-consuming process of filling out the lengthy application form. That approach was reinforced by random checks of the veracity of the declaration by social workers visiting the family home of the applicants and widespread publicity around the few cases of fraud brought to light by the social workers.

Assessing Policy Options to Anticipate Possible Consequences

Policy makers should rely on models and other analytic techniques to predict the direction and magnitude of the consequences of reforms. In addition, they can more easily identify problems early on and make the necessary adjustments thanks to adequate monitoring systems. Finally, they can protect financing reforms from political interference by strengthening the regulatory framework and institutional structure.

With regard to funding institutions, in some instances policies designed to achieve one goal may have unexpected, adverse consequences on another important objective. Countries such as the Netherlands, for example, have developed a performance-based funding formula in which institutions are paid for the number of students they graduate rather than the number of students they enroll. It is important to ensure that such a shift does not result in lower quality or grade inflation, as institutions seek to gain more funding by lowering their standards and graduating more students or allowing more students to complete their year of study. Another unintended consequence may be that institutions choose to compete more aggressively for the top-ranked students rather than seeking to improve the quality of the overall pool of students.

Over time, circumstances may change so much that the policy objectives reflected in the funding formula are no longer valid. The Polish experience is instructive in that regard. When the transition from a socialist to a market economy started in the early 1990s, policy makers realized that university coverage was quite low, as was the number of qualified teachers. Thus, the first funding formula elaborated at that time based the budget allocated to individual institutions on the number of students enrolled and the number of full-time faculty with a doctorate. This allocation model proved very effective in boosting the recruitment of full-time teaching staff with a doctorate. Fifteen years later, however, it had become a barrier for university departments wanting to hire part-time industry professionals without a doctorate as visiting professors. Unfortunately, the funding formula was inscribed in a higher education law voted by Parliament, making it difficult to adjust to changing circumstances.

Madagascar offers another illustration of a good reform turning bad after a few years for failure to monitor possible adverse consequences. As is the case with all Francophone tertiary education systems, spending on social benefits for students (subsidized meals, dormitories, transportation, and scholarships) was high until the early 1990s. In addition, managing these services is often a source of conflict, as students complain about the quality of the food, the conditions of their dormitories, or delays in the payment of scholarships. Thus, in the mid-1990s, the government decided to stop providing subsidized food services, which resulted in a significant decrease in social spending (scholarships, dormitories), from about 50 to 27 percent of the tertiary education budget. As a result, however, students in institutions that have dormitories started to use electric stoves, at the university's cost. This practice is so widespread that electricity costs now represent 42.5 percent of the total budget of the Ministry of Education's department responsible for social services. The electricity issue often becomes a source of conflicts with the students. In late 2006, students at the University of Antsiranana attacked and damaged the office of the president after the electricity company cut power to the university for lack of payment. As mentioned earlier, a similar situation arose again in May 2007 in the capital city when angry students from the engineering school (École Polytechnique) blocked the main road to the airport and were confronted by the army, with bloodshed narrowly avoided (Salmi 2008).

The sustainability of financing reforms can also be heavily influenced by government changes. In Togo, for example, one of the few Francophone African countries able to raise tuition fees in the early 2000s, the new government halved the fees in 2005. Similarly, in Senegal, the new minister of education reinstated universal scholarships in 2005 only two years after the previous administration had rationalized the eligibility criteria for scholarships and access to subsidized services (food and housing) to eliminate leakage.

Finally, the global financial crisis that started in late 2008 is likely to affect African economies in ways that will undoubtedly influence the availability of resources for tertiary education institutions. Declining economic activity will certainly result in budget reductions across the board. African universities, polytechnics, and colleges will certainly need to step up their fund-raising and cost-cutting efforts.

Thus, it is advisable to plan systematically for unanticipated consequences by relying on models and other analytic techniques that help to elaborate alternative scenarios to consider the possible direction and magnitude of these consequences, by setting up and using monitoring systems that allow policy makers to identify problems early on and make the necessary adjustments, and by strengthening the regulatory framework and institutional structure to protect financing reforms from political interference.

References

Altbach, Philip G. 1999. *Three Facets of Global Student Protest*. Boston: Boston College.

Bollag, Burton. 2003. *Improving Tertiary Education in Sub-Saharan Africa: Things That Work*. Washington, DC: World Bank.

Lao, Christine, and William Saint. 2009. "Legal Frameworks for Tertiary Education in Sub-Saharan Africa: The Quest for Institutional Responsiveness." Working Paper 175, World Bank, Washington, DC.

Salmi, Jamil. 2008. *Financing and Governance of Tertiary Education in Madagascar*. Washington, DC: World Bank.

Salmi, Jamil, and Arthur M. Hauptman. 2006. "Innovations in Tertiary Education Financing: A Comparative Evaluation of Allocation Mechanisms." Education Working Paper 4, World Bank, Washington, DC.

World Bank. 2002. *Constructing Knowledge Societies: New Challenges for Tertiary Education*. Washington, DC: World Bank.

ECO-AUDIT
Environmental Benefits Statement

The World Bank is committed to preserving endangered forests and natural resources. The Office of the Publisher has chosen to print *Financing Higher Education in Africa* on recycled paper with 30 percent post-consumer waste, in accordance with the recommended standards for paper usage set by the Green Press Initiative, a nonprofit program supporting publishers in using fiber that is not sourced from endangered forests. For more information, visit www.greenpressinitiative.org.

Saved:
- 7 trees
- 2 million BTU's of total energy
- 689 lbs of CO_2 equivalent of greenhouse gases
- 3,317 gallons of waste water
- 201 pounds of solid waste

www.ingramcontent.com/pod-product-compliance
Lightning Source LLC
Chambersburg PA
CBHW051928160426
43198CB00012B/2074